PRAISE FOR *TAKE 1*

"The knowledge revealed in Smokie Norful's book impressed me as much or even more than his multitude of recordings that impacted generations. His approach in challenging readers to look inward, outward, upward, and onward flows like the lyrics to one of his songs, inspiring you to leave your old life and anticipate the God-life where He makes all things new!"

—**Kirk Franklin**, *Grammy-winning recording artist*

"What you hold in your hand is an accelerator and capacity enhancer! My friend Smokie Norful has reached into his treasure chest of biblical revelation and shared precious jewels that unlock our understanding! Get ready to be stretched by God's thoughts concerning you!"

—**Bishop Dale C. Bronner**, *author and pastor, Word of Faith Family Worship Center, Atlanta, Georgia*

"Smokie Norful has penned a masterpiece that pushes us all beyond mediocrity and challenges us to pursue God's best for our lives. This book mirrors the life of a man who I know has taken the lid off and dared to be different. If you want the substance, strategies, and the story of success, this is a must read!"

—**Bishop Joseph W. Walker III**, *senior pastor, Mount Zion Baptist Church, Nashville, Tennessee; presiding bishop, Full Gospel Baptist Church Fellowship International*

"It is evident that God has blessed Smokie Norful with many gifts. In this awesome book, *Take the Lid Off,* Pastor Norful shares his personal life experiences, practical wisdom, and biblical principles that will help its readers understand the true benefits of God's unlimited power."

—**Bishop Paul S. Morton, Sr.**, *founder, Full Gospel Baptist Church Fellowship International; senior pastor, Changing a Generation Ministries, Atlanta, Georgia; overseer and copastor, Greater St. Stephen Ministries, New Orleans, Louisiana*

TAKE THE LID OFF

TAKE THE LID OFF

Trust God, Release the Pressure, and
Find the Life He Wants for You

SMOKIE NORFUL

NELSON
BOOKS
An Imprint of Thomas Nelson

Published in Nashville, Tennessee, by Nelson Books, anw imprint of Thomas Nelson. Nelson Books and Thomas Nelson are registered trademarks of HarperCollins Christian Publishing, Inc.

Thomas Nelson titles may be purchased in bulk for educational, business, fundraising, or sales promotional use. For information, please e-mail SpecialMarkets@ThomasNelson.com.

ISBN: 978-0-7180-9637-3 (TP)

Library of Congress Control Number: 2017936446

ISBN-13: 978-0-7180-7893-5

Printed in the United States of America

18 19 20 21 LSC 6 5 4 3 2 1

To my beautiful, super-strong, gifted, educated, intelligent, equipped, supportive, patient, unconditionally loving, compassionate, extraordinarily wise, calculating, funny, super-witty, gentle-spirited, persevering, loyal, faithful, dependable wife of twenty years, Carla Norful. Honestly, there are about a billion more descriptive words I could have used to describe all that you have been and are in my life. I love and appreciate you so much.

When I doubted myself—and yes, sometimes even God–you always pushed me to believe in Him and myself. Everyone sees and hears my voice on a regular basis not knowing that you are subtly and most profoundly my greatest cheerleader and the spark that keeps me getting back in the ring. And you do all this through your own selfless, gentle, and sometimes shy demeanor that causes people to think they've never heard you speak.

Well I know that they hear, see, and experience your prayers, encouragement, support, and power every time I grab a mic or pen to be used by God. In truth, your voice has helped mine be all it has been and it is you who helps me reach millions of people for the kingdom of God, just by reminding me that I can.

Now more than ever, I appreciate all the confidence you've had in me and all the faith you placed in my potential. Everything I have built and all I have achieved is because you believed in me. I once asked if you knew I would be all that I have become or do all I have been blessed to do when you married me. Your answer said it all, "I knew you had potential."

You are an incredible mother to our children, Tré, Ashton, and Ashley, and a dedicated, extraordinary wife. I am tremendously grateful to God for allowing me to share my life with you. This book is dedicated to you with the greatest heart of appreciation, admiration, and love. Thank you for loving and believing in me.

Emphatically, I praise God daily for my parents, W. R. and Teresa Norful Sr. Words cannot express my gratitude for you being the best parents anyone could have ever dreamed of having. I love you and appreciate all that you sacrificed for my brothers and me. I am because you are. *And you continue to amaze me with your undying love and support. I love you.*

Tré (God's Compassionate Leader), Ashton (God's Worshipping Warrior), and Ashley (God's Apologist and Theologian)—my children are among the most amazing, gifted, intellectual, and capable people I know. As much as I have taught and inspired you, you all have truly given me fifty times more. I learn from you daily. You make me a better father and person. I cannot wait to see how God uses you to do even greater works for the kingdom. Thank you for loving God and, more decisively, thank you for loving me. I love you with all my being, and I am honored to serve as covering, protector, confidante, leader, father, teacher, and student to each of you. Super-*proud to be your daddy!*

CONTENTS

PART 4: ONWARD

FOREWORD

A BABY IS BORN WITHOUT A LID.

Think about it this way. A baby is born with the software to learn any language spoken on this planet. If a baby is born in France, she will speak French. If the same baby is born in Brazil, she will speak Portuguese. That baby can learn any language. But very quickly, she is given her first lid. And then another. And then another.

Her parent's language, their accent, their life experiences, their financial margin, and even their thought processes, along with all the other human factors, start confining that baby—and lids start forming. She speaks her parents' language, thinks like them, and lives within their means. These are all lids.

And it doesn't stop there. As her life continues and she becomes a young lady, she starts placing additional lids and limitations on herself. These lids are self-imposed, hard to recognize, and difficult to change.

But there is good news for her and for you—we were born without lids, and we can live without them!

In *Take the Lid Off* my friend, Pastor Smokie Norful, identifies lids, how they form, and how to soar beyond them.

You will appreciate the candor and vulnerability in this book. You'll be nodding your head saying, "Me too!" You will connect instantly with the message—and even more with the recognition that you can trust God, release the pressure, and find the life He wants for you.

Take off the lid and soar.

—Samuel R. Chand,
leadership consultant and author of
Bigger, Faster Leadership
www.SamChand.com

INTRODUCTION

Our greatest fear should not be of
failure but of succeeding at things
in life that don't really matter.

—FRANCIS CHAN

MY GRANDMOTHER WAS AMAZING. SHE WAS BY FAR THE BEST COOK WHO EVER lived. She also thought I was something special. I'm not sure why, but I was the only child she let into her kitchen. It was her laboratory, and she didn't want anyone in her private domain—anyone but me, that is. In the kitchen, she was a chemist, an artist, and a poet. She could take ordinary ingredients (even scraps and leftovers) and turn them into a dish that a five-star restaurant would be proud to serve. Her specialty was "down-home cooking": fried catfish, candied yams, turnip greens, black-eyed peas, hot water cornbread, sweet potato pie, peach cobbler, and rice pudding. She lived in Arkansas, and at that time, our family lived in Oklahoma. We only visited my grandparents a few times a year, and I treasured those occasions.

When I was a boy, I had a special appreciation for my grandmother's talent in the kitchen. I loved her creativity, but even more, I enjoyed watching our family delight in consuming her edible creations. I always get a kick out of seeing people thrilled and satisfied with another person's creativity. As an adult, I feel deep joy when I see people listen to my music or get inspired by my preaching—and now, when they read my writing. It can all be traced back to the wonder of my grandmother's kitchen.

The dish I loved most was her sweet rice. Some people think rice only needs a little butter, salt, and pepper, but that's not our kind of rice. When my grandmother cooked it, she put a big dollop of butter right in the middle of the pot, and she poured in a large portion of pure cane sugar. That's the way we liked our lemonade, iced tea, and rice—syrupy sweet!

One day, I walked up behind my grandmother in the kitchen and boldly said, "I'd like you to teach me how to cook rice. Would you show me?" She waved me to come up beside her and said, "I sure will. You just do everything I do. Watch really close." She showed me every step she took, from beginning to end, to make her sweet rice. When we finished cooking, the result was indescribably delicious!

Two days later I walked into the kitchen early in the morning to find my grandmother already in there. Before I said a word, she announced, "Today's your day. You are going to make rice!" I had been in rice-cooking boot camp, and it was finally time for me to show my stuff.

She got out the ingredients for me, but that was the extent of her contribution. She had already shown me how to do it, and now it was time for me to practice the skills she had demonstrated. My grandmother and I were the only people awake that early in the morning; therefore, I had no distractions. She walked over to the other side of the kitchen and began preparing homemade rolls, peas, and other dishes to serve for dinner that evening.

I followed each step I'd watched her perform two days before.

I thought things were going well—exceptionally well, in fact—but my thrill was tempered by a nagging doubt in the back of my mind that I might have forgotten a crucial step. From time to time, my grandmother walked over and gazed at my creation in progress. Like God on the days of creation, she pronounced, "It is good." Each time she walked by with her affirmation, I felt a little better.

The rice was simmering nicely when I thought it would be a good idea to put a lid on the pot to keep all the goodness from escaping in steam. I found a lid that fit and put it on. I turned and walked over to where my grandmother was slicing potatoes and onions. As we talked, we both heard a faint hissing sound. It got louder. Suddenly, I realized it was coming from my pot of rice! I yelled, "Grandma, I'm burning the house down!"

I ran over to the stove, turned around, and hollered, "What should I do?"

She said clearly and firmly, "Just take the lid off!"

I didn't understand. I was sure I was supposed to have a lid on the rice. I answered, "What do you mean?"

Her eyes opened wide, and she repeated, in no uncertain terms, "Take the lid off!"

I snatched the lid off. It was hot, so I dropped it near the pot. The wildly boiling water quickly went back down to a simmer. Water from the pot had run down the sides of the pot and formed little lakes on the top of the stove, but the rice was saved. No irreparable harm done.

I looked back over at my grandmother. She just smiled and nodded. She knew this was only a small error in my cooking debut. A few minutes later, the rest of the family came into the kitchen. (I don't know if they heard all the shouting, but they were smiling and nodding to each other when they walked in.) Together, we enjoyed delicious sweet rice—*my* delicious sweet rice. From that day on, it became my signature dish. (For several years it was my *only* dish.) No matter who came over to our house or what the occasion might be, I always offered to cook a pot of sweet rice.

Sometimes our lives are like that sealed pot of rice in my grandmother's kitchen: hissing, boiling over, about to explode, and creating panic. In those tense moments, we need to take the lid off. When we do, the pressure subsides, allowing us to gain peace and perspective, leading to a better outcome.

Many of us are slow learners. We've mistakenly put a lid on our lives and lived with the tension of built-up pressure for years. The pressure builds when our full potential isn't being released into the world. It manifests as tension when we're not living the life God has in store for us. When our covered "pot" is boiling out of control, the steam of trapped potential is hissing, puddles of problems gather around us, and we become so frustrated we don't know what to do! If we leave the lid on our lives, we run the risk of ruining what's in the pot—our relationships, our dreams, and our goals—and stress will rob us of creativity and joy. Our self-confidence will be crushed, and others will begin to say disheartening things to us and about us. Fear and doubt will consume our thoughts, and we'll conclude we'll never be able to see our dreams realized or make anything of our lives. Everything in the pot will be ruined—or at least, so it will seem to be.

Perhaps people in our past have instructed us on various ways to take the lid off, but we didn't listen. We thought we knew how to "cook our lives" and make them delicious and inspiring, but we were wrong. Now is the time to listen. We've seen the damage and heard the hissing long enough. It is now time to do something! Take the lid off. It is never too late. God is a God of second chances (and third and fourth chances too). He delights when people finally turn to Him, experience His grace and forgiveness, take the lid off their lives, and experience the joy, power, and peace of a life well lived.

Some of us have lived with the lid on so long that we can't imagine life without it. But it is possible. In fact, God promises abundance when we finally turn to Him. Jesus said, "I have come that they may have life, and have it to the full" (John 10:10). What does it mean to live a full, abundant life? Jesus was saying that we need to take the lid off to reveal the unlimited potential of being God's children. Most of us live with the lid on our lives—glued on, stuck on, or welded tight. We're trapped in a boiling pot of broken hearts and shattered dreams. We hiss in our resentment and self-pity, but we don't do anything productive to solve the problem. Day after day, we just boil till we overflow in anger, shame, blame, and frustration. When we finally take the lid off, we can more fully engage in the life God has created for us and live out the potential we were intended to fulfill. With our "lids off" we are in closer contact with the unlimited power of His Spirit. This divine contact challenges us to live a life of inspired, holy purpose where we can experience the joy of seeing Him transform us and then act as change agents in the lives of others.

THE FOURFOLD FOCUS

All of us need help in taking the lid off. That's what this book is about: providing a clear plan for removing the lid from our lives. Each pair of chapters focuses on a different element of doing so: the inward, the outward, the upward, and the onward.

When we look *inward*, we experience the cleansing of forgiveness, the power of the Holy Spirit, and the purpose to advance God's kingdom. We can't be of any use to God or have a positive impact on others if our hearts are boiling—or empty because everything good has boiled out. We won't be an asset to God or to our families, businesses, schools, and churches if we don't get our inward lives in order.

But this is not enough. One of the most common mistakes people make is to focus entirely on their own goals, desires, and wants. God, however, wants us to have an *outward* focus. When we are self-absorbed, we miss the joy of being a blessing to others. Being self-centered stifles opportunities to allow God to remove limitations that allow us to have the abundant life He promises us. Taking the lid off also means wanting others to experience the joy of living for God and having the best God has to offer. Jesus Himself came to serve, not to be served. As He fills our hearts, we will increasingly and joyfully serve others instead of demanding to be the center of attention. In fact, we can only find and follow our true potential by giving ourselves away to help others reach their full potential. Actually, this is one of the most important keys to reaching your full potential.

Too often, we're self-absorbed as well as self-sufficient (or at least we act as if we are self-sufficient). We may go to church, read our Bibles, and pray, but then we walk away and often live as if God doesn't exist. Some of us have become "practical atheists." We need a fresh perspective: the only source of meaning is God's will; the only source of love is the heart of God; and the only unlimited power in the universe is God's mighty hand. We need to look *upward* and marvel at God's love, forgiveness, and power. Our *vertical* relationship with God determines the outcome of all our *horizontal* goals, dreams, and connections. Jesus said, "Seek first the kingdom of

God" (Matt. 6:33 NKJV)—not second or third, but *first.* The psalmist asked and answered an important question: "I lift up my eyes to the mountains—where does my help come from? My help comes from the LORD, the Maker of heaven and earth" (Ps. 121:1–2). The mountains in our lives might be threats or opportunities. Either way, our help comes from the Lord.

When our *inward* hearts are full of the love of God, and our eyes are focused *outward* on the needs of others instead of ourselves, and we have mastered looking *upward,* trusting in God's love and strength to accomplish His purposes, we're ready to move *onward.* Now it's time to put God's plans into practice. It's not enough to sit on the sidelines and watch others take the lids off their potential. We need to devise a strategy to accomplish all God has put in our hearts to do. God has given each of us spiritual gifts, and He expects us to use them—not to shine a light on ourselves, but to shine a bright light on His purpose and plans. Many people miss this point. They spend time trying to get their hearts full, and they dabble in serving here and there, but they don't experience the sheer joy of seeing God use them to answer the prayer, "Your kingdom come. Your will be done on earth as it is in heaven" (Matt. 6:10 NKJV). The fourth element of taking the lid off calls us to partner with God and bring people from the domain of darkness into the light of God's Son.

MY HOPE FOR YOU

God has been waiting for you to take the lid off. He wants to drench you with the abundance of His love, grace, joy, and power. I hope you're ready! I pray that you'll understand God's divine will for your life and experience the power of the Spirit to reach your full potential.

In Paul's second letter to the Corinthians, he wanted to blow the doors off their imaginations. Paul understood that their minds could not comprehend all that God wanted to do in them, for them, and through them. He wrote, "And God is able to make all grace abound to you, so that in all things at all times, having all that you need, you will abound in every good work" (2 Cor. 9:8 NIV 1984). The same message applies to us today. Don't miss this: *all* grace, at *all* times, in *all* we need, for *everything* we do—no exceptions!

Don't let anything keep you from God's best. Try Him, and experience more fulfillment, delight, power, and success than you ever dreamed. That's what God wants for you. Don't wait any longer. *Take the lid off!*

The mystery of human existence lies not in just staying alive, but in finding something to live for.

—FYODOR DOSTOYEVSKY

PART 1

INWARD

ONE

ALL OR NOTHING

If you want the fire of God, you
must become the fuel of God.

—TOMMY TENNEY

I'M NOT SURE IF IT'S A BLESSING OR A CURSE, BUT I'M AN ALL-OR-NOTHING KIND of guy. I'm not satisfied with half measures and partial attempts. When I step into a venture, I believe it has vast potential, and I won't settle for anything less. When I taught history in high school, I didn't see my role starting and stopping when the bell rang. If a student had a consistent problem with truancy, I went over to his house to wake him up and take him to school on time. On Sunday morning, I went to his house to take him to church. And this wasn't just one student. I did this for many kids in my classroom. The students (and their parents) sensed that I was giving them everything I had, and they appreciated my commitment to them.

Over the years God has tempered me, so I'm a little more cautious. (It only takes a few impulsive and colossal mistakes to get my attention!) Now, I weigh things very carefully before I sign on because once I'm committed, I'm in all the way.

Sometimes, however, God's "all" is vastly different from our "all."

When I began my music career, I had no idea how much favor

God would pour out on me. It was humbling and astounding. By the grace of God, I am a successful recording artist. My albums have risen to the top of the charts and remained there. I was *Billboard* magazine's number-one recording artist in gospel music two years in a row. My albums had sold more in this genre than any other artist's during this period. The critics noticed. I won award after award: two Grammys, three Stellars, four Doves, and more. Two of my albums went gold, and eventually, I sold platinum (one million). I was asked to sing on five national fund-raising programs, jazz festivals, and awards shows—the pre-Grammy show, the Dove Awards, the Parade of Stars, the BET awards, and many others—more than I can remember. All the while I was saying to myself, *I'm just a young man from the plains of central Arkansas—this has to be God!* All of this was happening because of the matchless favor of God. To Him be all the glory!

In 2005 I was at the pinnacle of my career, and it looked very promising for the future. One day, it was as if I had turned a corner and come across a stop sign. I sensed the Lord say to me, *Okay, now it's time.*

I reacted. "Time for what?"

I had everything any artist could ever dream of enjoying: money, celebrity, creativity, opportunity, and realized potential. When I wasn't performing, I served in the local church. My wife, Carla, and our kids were doing great. During these years, I walked with God, trusting Him and giving Him honor at every point in my career. I resisted the temptation to live for fame and wealth, and God gave me wisdom and strength to stay strong when I faced unjust criticism and betrayal. Everything was perfect. I was living the dream—*but I was miserable!*

Shortly after hearing God's deafening words, "Now it's time," I stopped going to church. Imagine that. I was a PK (preacher's kid). I grew up on the front row of the church, sang God's praises, accepted my call to preach, and attended seminary. God had blessed me with incredible favor in my music career. All of this was wonderful and meaningful, but I had a nagging sense that something was very wrong. Peace and joy had vanished from my life. Going to church made me feel empty, but I had no idea why. My remedy was to avoid church . . . and avoid God.

From the outside—and from my perspective—my discouragement and disillusionment made no sense at all. God had opened magnificent doors of opportunity, and He'd blessed me beyond measure. I believed I was doing exactly what He had called me to do, which was to sing about the wonders of His glory and grace. I had delighted myself in God, and He had blessed me with the desires of my heart to reach countless people with the musical talents He had given me. People from every race, age, and socioeconomic group wrote me to say how much my music inspired them. God had given me His all. Yet, though my life had every appearance of giving God *my* all, I hadn't really given it all to Him. I still clung to certain facets of my life, and I wanted to stay in control of those things. As a result, my peace had vanished.

When we hold something back, our hearts know it . . . and God knows it. We experience the fullness of God's perfect peace only when we're fully surrendered to His will and when we delight more in Him than in His gifts.

During this time, God sent His Spirit and my mother to point the way. Every Sunday morning, my mother called me. With a stern voice that sounded as if she were scolding a misbehaving child, she asked, "Are you up? Are you getting ready for church? You're going to church today, aren't you?"

I tried to ignore her. In my mind, I justified not going to church because I'd been traveling so much—and after all, I was singing about God! Quite often, I was out of town on Sundays; therefore, I had a good excuse (or so I thought). But when I was at home, I still found reasons to stay in bed. It was my day off. Every Sunday, Carla took our children, Tré and Ashton, to church while I stayed home, feeling distant from God and sorry for myself.

When I didn't give God my all, I lost my peace. Though I didn't lose my favor, my family, or my life, I realize the result of being distant from God could have been worse. God's grace and mercy continued to protect me because He had bigger and better plans for me—even when I didn't see them, and even when I didn't pursue Him.

One day, I finally realized that I'd been ignoring God's best plan for me. It had taken a lot of messages to get through to me: from my mother, my wife, the Spirit of God, my lack of peace, and a nagging sense that God was calling me to be something else—a pastor. There were plenty of warnings and encouragements. Finally, God got through to me. It dawned on me that I'd confused God's blessing for God's purposes. Finally, I understood: God's future purposes are always bigger than God's present blessings. So, I came up with a solution. Since God wanted me to be involved in teaching the Scriptures and discipling people, I decided to start a Bible study.

I was in a recording studio in Memphis, working on a new album with two of my team members at the time. I told my music director, Jason Tyson, that God was leading me to start a Bible study when I returned to Chicago. He was surprised but supportive. During a break, I called my friend, recording artist Donnie McClurkin, to tell him my plans for the Bible study. I was excited because I felt I was finally doing what God wanted. I was sure he would be excited too. I was wrong.

He quickly asked, "Smokie, why are you doing that?"

I was shocked. I thought he'd be supportive and enthusiastic when he heard my plans. Instead, he was skeptical. I explained (a little defensively), "I'm walking in my anointing. I'm going to teach the Word of God!"

He didn't budge. He asked again, "But why are you doing it?"

Now I was really confused. I told him, "Because God told me to teach a Bible study, that's why." He didn't say a word. After a long, awkward pause, I continued. "I've been to seminary. I'm prepared, and I've acknowledged God's call on my life to teach the Scriptures and lead people. I taught and preached for years, and now it's time to get back to this calling."

I was sure my sterling logic was thoroughly convincing, yet Donnie sounded frustrated, as if I hadn't been listening to him when he asked his question. Again, he asked me, "Yes, Smokie. I understand all that, but *why* are you going to lead a Bible study?"

I explained again. "Because this is the way I'm going to prove to God that I haven't abandoned His call on my life."

Donnie quickly asked, "Did God tell you to do it?"

I wasn't sure how to respond, so I told him, "Well, yeah, of course. The Bible says, 'Preach the word in season and out of season.'[1] This is my season."

He had me. He asked, "Smokie, did God tell you to start a Bible study, or did He tell you to pastor people and preach His Word in a church?"

His words triggered a holy moment. I felt like Isaiah, who had stood in front of God's throne and heard the very words of God. The Spirit used Donnie's voice to speak words of grace and truth to my heart. Suddenly I realized I'd missed God's will again. I didn't want to be inconvenienced or have my comfort level altered, so I assumed God wanted me to lead a Bible study. Reluctantly, I began to understand that leading a Bible study was still only a half measure, a partial commitment. I was still holding back from giving every fiber of my being.

I sensed the Spirit say, *"I know you hear Me."*

Yes, I heard Him, but I didn't want to become a pastor. I wanted to stay in control of my options, my life, and my career. My desires were making me miserable, but I still wanted to hold them tight. I didn't want to trust God with my whole heart.

I'd like to say that I joyfully accepted God's directive, but I didn't. I thought of every excuse in the book instead of listening to Donnie's wise advice on the phone. I thought, *I can't do that. . . . I'm too young. . . . I can't preach to people who are as old as my grandmother. . . . I don't have time. . . . I'm already pressed to do everything now, and being a pastor is a consuming, never-ending role. . . . My schedule is already packed with things God has given me to do. . . . I can't neglect God's obvious blessings. No, it just won't work. . . . I don't know enough. Yes, I've been to seminary, but I have so much more to learn about the Bible, spiritual life, and leading people. . . . Where will the money come from to start a church? I have the resources, but I have another plan for those resources. . . . Maybe in the future I'll know enough, have enough resources for church planting, and have plenty of time to devote to being a pastor. . . . No, this can't be what God is calling me to do.* There wasn't an excuse I didn't try to use!

The reasons in my head sounded so good that I was sure they'd convince Donnie. I listed them one by one and presented my case to him. For each one, he wore me out with piercing passages of Scripture. He had an answer for everything—and not just his own ideas. He used God's Word to refute every excuse! He talked about David's youth, Jonah's running, Paul's persecution, Peter's repentance, and

Jesus' sacrifice to do the Father's will no matter the cost. He cut me no slack. I had no rebuttal. By the time he had finished, my excuses had fallen in a heap on the floor.

Donnie's piercing truths made me weep. Through my sobs, I thanked him for being such a good friend, and I hung up. When I went back into the studio, I was still bawling. The guys in the studio looked at me and wondered who had died! They ran over to me and began asking questions: "What happened, Smokie?" "What's wrong?" "What can we do?" "What's going on?"

I couldn't get any words to come out of my mouth. I just nodded and forced a smile to show them I was okay. Finally, I mumbled, "I just need some time to pray." Immediately the recording session stopped and we joined together in prayer. The group still thought a family member had died. Jason went to the piano and began playing a beautiful, calming melody. When I heard the music, the words *I'll say yes* leaped into my spirit. Jason, unknowingly, was being used by God to speak to my stubborn spirit. My prayer of surrender suddenly transformed into extemporaneous song lyrics:

> I'll say yes to whatever it is You want me to be.
> *I'll say yes to whatever it is You would have for me*
> *I'll live out Your purpose; I'll give You my whole heart*
> *For I know now, there's nothing too hard for my God,*
> *I'll say yes.*

I was singing through my sobs. Soon, tears began to flow all around the room. My friends didn't even know why they were crying, but they loved me so much that they identified with me in that sensitive moment of pain and surrender.

My prayer song ended, and we all sat in silence. Finally, I took a deep breath and said, "I have to pastor." They knew this wasn't a flippant comment. My declaration was washed in tears and animated by renewed commitment to God's purpose.

I left the recording studio eager to begin plans to start a church in the Chicago area. I quickly realized I knew nothing about church planting. My father was a pastor, but he had always served in established churches, so I was never exposed to this specific type of leadership as a child. But I knew God wanted me to do something new and that He would guide me through the process.

When I got back home, I started searching the community to find a place to meet. I went to libraries, schools, banks, and every other place that might have a meeting room that would be empty on Sunday mornings. My plans were rudimentary, but God was in them all. At the beginning, I was a one-man show. I was the worship leader, the pastor, the head usher, the greeter, the one who read the announcements, and the janitor who cleaned up after each service. I enlisted my wife, Carla, and my kids to help, and they were glad to pitch in wherever they could.

Soon, though, I began to feel overwhelmed. A member who had been one of the first to join realized I was in over my head and said, "Dr. Derrick Hughes, a friend of mine, helps pastors plant churches. Would you like to talk to him?"

No, I didn't want to talk to him. I wanted to have his brain transplanted into mine! This man was like an angel sent from heaven. He knew how to conduct a demographic study of the community, how to find resources, how to set up leadership, how to make an initial impression on potential church members, how to build bridges with civic leaders and other pastors, and how to do all this without dropping dead from exhaustion! He was an incredible help. In the formative days, weeks, and months when we planted our church,

I lived the message of the hymn: "All I have needed, Thy hand has provided—Great is Thy faithfulness, Lord, unto me!"[2] When I said yes to God, He gave me everything I needed to fulfill His purposes—but not immediately, and not easily. The process of discovery and testing was part of God's curriculum for me to learn and grow as a pastor. It was all part of His plan.

YOUR GIFTING, YOUR CALLING

I'm not suggesting that being fully devoted to God—being all-in—means a person has to become a pastor or a missionary or find some other kind of vocational Christian service. During the Reformation, Martin Luther had two sweeping messages. First, he taught that salvation is purely and only a gift of God's grace; there's no way we can earn it by being good enough, giving enough money, or being zealous enough to impress God. It's all about grace. His second message isn't as well known, but it's very important. In Luther's day, people believed there were two categories of Christians: (1) the first-class Christians, who became professionals in the church, and (2) the second-class Christians, who worked in factories, fields, and homes. Luther said that's not the way God has created the world. He taught the revolutionary concept that every job, role, and responsibility is valuable to God. The person who works in the fields *is* doing God's work just as much as the person behind the pulpit. He called it "the priesthood of all believers." This means that when we become fully devoted to Christ, He may lead us to a different job, but more often He makes us shine like bright lights of His truth and grace where we already live and work. Every believer is called to represent God all day every day. Os Guinness wrote that our calling is "the truth that God calls us to himself so decisively that everything we are, everything we do, and everything we have is invested with a special devotion and dynamism lived out as a response to his summons and service."[3]

We need to get our priorities straight. Our first calling isn't to a role or a job; it's to God Himself. When the love and power of God flow *into* us and overflow *from* us, the resulting flood of grace has a powerful impact on everyone around us—in our homes, at work, in our neighborhoods, and in our churches. God has a unique path for each of us. It's our challenge and privilege to discover it and follow it to His glory.

Every person's calling is to be fully devoted to Jesus Christ. Paul told the believers in Philippi that God was at work in them "to will and to act according to his good purpose." As they put their hands in His, God promised to make them "blameless and pure, 'children of God without fault in a crooked and depraved generation,'" in which they would shine like stars in the universe (Phil. 2:13, 15 NIV 1984). Whoever we are and whatever we do, we can shine like stars to everyone who's watching. All of us are priests, ministers, and servants of the King. No exceptions.

"Well, that's all fine," people often tell me, "but I'm confused. How can I find God's will for my life?" God has given us powerful directives and supportive resources. We find God's will by the combination of God's Word, God's Spirit, and God's people. The Bible tells us very clearly about right and wrong in many important areas of life: don't commit adultery; instead, love and respect your spouse. Don't steal; instead, work hard to earn a living and give generously. Don't harbor bitterness; instead, forgive just as Christ has forgiven you. These commands (and many others) are clear and unmistakable. The Bible, though, doesn't tell us to take this job or that one. We need the leading of the Spirit to show us the way. The Spirit of God isn't an impersonal force. He's a person, part of the Trinity. He is our Counselor, and when we suffer, He prays for us "with groanings too deep for words" (Rom. 8:26 ESV). The Spirit illumines the Scriptures so we understand them better, and He whispers for us to go in a particular direction. He leads us in a process of uncovering our desires, identifying our talents, and finding opportunities. Even then, we may not know which way to go until God sends someone to give us confirmation or correction. God uses all of these, sometimes dramatically, but more often slowly and subtly in a process of discovery. Sometimes, he even uses a friend like Donnie McClurkin to challenge our motives and direction.

God *wants* our all. More important, He *deserves* our all. Jesus didn't merely offer to give us some assistance; He gave His all as a sacrifice in our place. We are so sinful that it took the death of the Son of God to pay for our sins. When we surrender our hearts, our lives, our futures, and our resources to Him, it's only a dim reflection of all He has given to us. Our gifts to Him are always flawed in some way because we are deeply flawed people. We depended on His grace on the first day we decided to trust Him, and we still bask in His grace all day, every day. We never have leverage on God. We never pull His strings. It's all grace, first to last. We will never *do* enough to earn His favor. Isaac Watts's beloved hymn reminds us of our responsibility upon receiving this gift: "Love so amazing, so divine, demands my soul, my life, my all."[4]

Even when God was blessing me so much, I still didn't give Him my all. He gave me the desires of my heart—more abundantly than I ever dreamed possible—but I was still too apathetic, too lukewarm, too full of doubts, and too self-absorbed to be fully engaged with

Him. Even then, God didn't turn His back on me, and He didn't give up on me. He took my sin and cast it into the deepest sea of forgetfulness, and then He whispered, "*Smokie, come back to Me. I have so much more for you. Will you come? I love you. Please come back!*" God is omniscient, so He can't forget anything, but He chose not to hold my sins against me. That's what it means when the Bible says that God forgets.[5] To Him, it's as if it never happened. When I ponder the depth of His forgiveness when I was so selfish, I love Him even more.

EXCUSES AND COP-OUTS

Human beings are created by God and for God, but sin has messed up everything. The default mode of the human heart is self-sufficiency and self-indulgence. We want what we want, and we don't want to depend on anybody else. Even when we realize God wants to shower us with His favor, we find excuses to walk away from Him. We use any reason to cop out of the purpose we were created to enjoy: to know, love, and follow Jesus Christ.

Many people are distracted from God's promises and purposes. They make a good-faith effort to come to church and sing the songs, but their minds often drift to things that seem much more important: which team will win the game that afternoon, the grocery list, rehashing an argument with their spouses on the way to church, or a host of other distractions. At home, they're distracted thinking about all the things they have to do at work; at work, they're distracted thinking about all the problems, needs, and demands at home. Distractions are everywhere!

When our minds wander, we don't think enough about the

phenomenal, life-changing truths of the Bible concerning the cross and resurrection, the hope of the gospel, and the wonder of God's love. Some of us think "the abundant Christian life" is merely about attending church. With that mind-set, we fail to experience a faith in Christ that connects us to the greatest love, the greatest power, and the greatest adventure on the planet! Ignorance begins as a legitimate problem, but sooner or later, it becomes a *willful* choice. People hide behind *not knowing* as an excuse for *not obeying.*

A second reason people don't go all-in for God is because of fear. It manifests in many different forms, and like a deadly acid, it corrodes our passion for God. Some are afraid God won't come through when they need Him. Some live in fear that the people they love and value will ridicule them, or that their families will disown them. Certainly, going all-in with God contains some risks. Adventures always involve risks! The question, of course, is, is the risk worth it? Is the potential gain worth the risk we take in any venture, including the venture of following Christ wherever He leads us? The answer is *yes!* It's absolutely worth it.

Other people look at their limited resources and conclude, "Really, I can't do much for God." They feel inadequate. They believe they don't have the right academic degree or professional connections. But they're missing the point. When God calls us to love Him and follow Him with all our hearts, souls, and strength, He doesn't leave us to depend on *our* resources. We have access to *His* incomparable resources! The prefix to the word *resource* is *re,* which means "again." We don't need to look at our resources. Instead, we need to focus on our ultimate, unlimited, omnipotent source: God, the Creator and Sustainer of all things. In Psalm 24, King David reminds us:

> The earth is the Lord's, and everything in it,
> the world, and all who live in it;
> for he founded it on the seas
> and established it on the waters. (vv. 24:1–2)

Some people say, "Well, I earn my paycheck. God didn't supply that." Think about it. Where do our talents come from? God has given them to us. Who is the Source of our life and breath? God. Who has given us the open doors to use our abilities? God. He is the Author of life, the Creator of the universe, and the Lover of our souls. Everything we have comes from His gracious hand—for believers and unbelievers alike. In the book of Matthew, Jesus told the crowd about the Father's generosity: "He causes his sun to rise on the evil and the good, and sends rain on the righteous and the unrighteous" (5:45).

When we look at the Source, we realize what we have in our hands is nothing compared to all God can bring to bear for those who trust Him. God will bring all the resources of heaven and earth to us when we trust Him in the proper timing. If we need networking connections, He brings a wise person into our lives. When we need wisdom, He leads us to a book, a mentor, or a seminar. When we need a skilled staff member or volunteer, He knows how to coordinate the events so our paths cross. When we need tangible resources, God tests us to see if we really trust Him, often making us wait in faith. Sooner or later, though, He provides what we need. He is Jehovah-Jireh, the Lord Who Provides.

Too often, we want God to provide, but only to meet our needs and fulfill our wants. We are consumers in every other part of our lives, and we are consumers in our relationship with God too. We want our way, not His. We expect Him to fulfill our expectations instead of leading us to serve others. Yes, we come to God empty and hope to be filled, but the filling isn't an end in itself. When God fills us, we have the responsibility of pouring ourselves into others to bless them with the blessings we've received. For many of us, the pipeline of blessing is plugged with selfishness. Humility, brokenness, and repentance unplug the pipe and clear the way for the flow of favor.

God does not single people out as His favorites, but He freely pours His favor on all who do His will. He grants us favor in three distinct ways. First, He protects us from harm, sickness, and evil. Unknowingly, His hand has often shielded us from catching a disease, being in a fatal car wreck, or countless other possible calamities. Second, His favor can shower us with success, healing, restoration, and other tangible blessings. The third way He shows His favor is by giving us the faith, courage, patience, and endurance to walk with Him in the midst of our struggles. That, too, is evidence of the power and grace of God in our lives.

God is searching, looking, and waiting for people to trust in Him for direction and strength. The prophet Hanani told King Asa, "For the eyes of the LORD range throughout the earth to strengthen those whose hearts are fully committed to him" (2 Chron. 16:9). When He looks, does He find me? Does He find you? When He finds those who are totally surrendered, He unleashes the full blessings of heaven on them!

When God spoke to me through my friend Donnie, I made plenty of excuses. My fears were in overdrive! But God touched my heart, broke my willfulness, and gave me His assurance that following Him into the unknown was the most reasonable thing I could ever do. If I didn't say yes, I would have missed out on the greatest blessings of my life, and I wouldn't have the incredible privilege of seeing God use me, our church, and our expanded ministry to shine like stars in our community, our country, and the world. To God be all the glory!

THE COST

Every choice is a value statement, and every decision has a price tag. When we surrender our hearts and our lives to God, we have to count the costs in two ways: internally and externally. In the depths of our souls, we have to make a calculation. Do we value the glory and purposes of God more than we do our selfish desires? Or, do our wants win the contest? This isn't a light and easy question. It's a call to die—nothing less and nothing else. Over and over in the Gospels, Jesus predicted His death to ransom captured souls. But He also explained that everyone who follows Him would have to make the same decision to die. To die for Christ means to surrender, to say no to selfish demands and yes to Christ's invitation to love Him more than anything or anyone and obey Him no matter the cost.

What does this choice look like? Instead of comfort, we choose sacrifice. Instead of bitterness, we choose to forgive. Instead of fame, we give glory to God. Instead of status and positions, we choose to humbly serve. All of these call us to put our selfish desires to death for a greater Person, a greater cause, and a greater reward.

If only choosing God's will instead of our own comfort, power, control, and fame came naturally—but it doesn't. Most of us cling to those things as long as we possibly can. Sooner or later, God allows us to be touched by heartache, failure, or shame (Jer. 29:11)—enough so that we come to the end of ourselves and reach out to Him in desperate faith. That's the pivotal point of brokenness. It's painful, but it's essential. Every great man or woman of God in the Bible and throughout history has had to come to that point of decision, and for most, it comes only through the experience of pain.

We face points of decision every day. Paul called our bodies a "living sacrifice" (Rom. 12:1–2), which means we sometimes want to climb down off the altar! Our choices either put God first or feed our selfish desires. These choices are the external cost we pay. They are as varied as personality, gifting, age, and responsibility. We *choose* to listen to someone who is boring instead of showing contempt and walking away. We *choose* to affirm someone who has ignored or criticized us instead of taking verbal revenge. We *choose* to help a stranger when our schedules are already full.

The external cost of giving our all to God ranges from sacrificing a little time to giving our entire lives. When God reorients our priorities, we might choose to get up thirty minutes early to read the Bible and pray. Most of the time, it's a matter of giving up some comforts to help those around us. Sometimes, though, the external costs are much more than a minor inconvenience. Some of us suffer ridicule and estrangement from our families when we choose to follow Christ with all our hearts. We thought they'd applaud; instead, they condemn us. They accuse us of being radical and foolish for putting God first. That's been the steepest cost for me. Some people who supported me in my music career were less than encouraging when I followed God's leading to be a pastor. I used to have more time to hang out with them. Now, when I can't go to social events because I have to prepare a sermon or care for a hurting person, they complain that I'm not as good a friend and not as much fun as I used to be. Even worse, some say I'm too religious. I try to explain that God has a hold on the priorities of my life. I'm not my own; I've been bought with a price. But they just shake their heads and give a look of disdain. To them, I've become strange and distant. Sometimes it would be easier to give in to their demands, but turning my back on God incurs a far higher cost that I'm not willing to pay.

Some of us pay the cost at work. We come home at a reasonable hour to spend time with our spouses and children instead of staying at work until nine o'clock. Our bosses notice, and promote the person who sacrificed his faith and his family to get ahead at work.

But make no mistake: There's always a cost in time, money, convenience, energy, reputation, relationships, and life itself. When we say we "follow Jesus," it means we follow His example of putting the Father's purposes above our own, even to the point of giving our lives for God and for others. And that hurts. Sacrifice and suffering are essential parts of the abundant life. That can hurt. These experiences expose our true passions, reveal our values, and give us opportunities to follow in the Master's footsteps. When we're broken, we become pliable and useful in God's hands. Pastor and author A. W. Tozer observed, "It is doubtful that God can use a man greatly until He hurts him deeply."[6]

In the book of Luke, Jesus was very clear about the cost of following Him . . . and the impotence of excuses. One man told Him, "I will follow you wherever you go." He was saying, "I'm all in," but Jesus raised the bar. He told the man, "That sounds good, but you don't really get it yet. If you want to follow me, you have to be willing to give up everything, even your creature comforts." He explained, "Foxes have holes and birds of the air have nests, but the Son of Man has no place to lay his head."

Jesus turned to a second man and said, "Follow me." This guy wasn't ready. He had his own agenda. He put his family ahead of God. He made the excuse that he had to go home and take care of his father. How long? Until his father died. Jesus didn't buy that excuse. He told him, "Let the dead bury their own dead, but you go and proclaim the kingdom of God."

A third man expressed his commitment to follow Jesus, but with a condition: he wanted to go home and say good-bye to his family. Jesus saw through his excuse. He told the man, "No one who puts a hand to the plow and looks back is fit for service in the kingdom of God" (9:57–62).

Was Jesus being harsh? Was He unreasonable? No, we are created and crafted by God, and we function best when we are fully devoted to Him alone. Our families are tremendously important, but they come after our devotion to God. If we put anything else ahead of God, we end up leaning on it too much, getting our identity from it, and eventually sucking the life out of it. If we are more devoted to our careers than to God, money and promotions become too important. Our jobs can't save us from sin, and they can't give us ultimate fulfillment. Only God can do that. We can appropriately love our families and enjoy our work only when we put first things first—and God is the *ultimate* and *only* first. Has He earned that place in our lives? He is the Creator, King, and Savior. Everything we have comes from His gracious hand, He rules over all with sovereignty and wisdom, and we'd be completely lost without His saving grace.

REAL TRANSFORMATION

The answer isn't to try to become more devoted, passionate, or zealous to prove ourselves to God. Instead, we look at the sacrifice of Jesus. He stepped out of the perfection, beauty, and glory of heaven; became a servant; and suffered ridicule, torture, and murder, all so you and I can be rescued from sin and adopted into God's own family. Jesus took the righteous judgment we deserve, and God gave us the honor Jesus deserves. Paul said that Jesus became sin—the thing He hates the most—to pay the full price for it. And in its place, He has clothed us with His own righteousness (2 Cor. 5:21). We know the measure of love by what it gives. Jesus gave up His comfort, His status, His authority, and His life—not because He had to, but because He wanted to. We were once God's enemies. Now we are beloved sons and daughters of the King. Yeah, I'd say He deserves our love and devotion!

In the Roman Empire in the first century, communication was a bit slower than it is today—no Internet, cell phones, Instagram, Twitter, or Facebook. When the authorities wanted to get news out to the people, they posted a message, an imperial edict, or a decree in the center of town by nailing it high on a post. At the moment it was nailed to the post, the new law went into effect. When Jesus was nailed to the post in Jerusalem, His new message—God's imperial decree—went into effect. Ironically, Jesus' enemies nailed Him to the cross. This was an act that announced the once-and-for-all Good News of the forgiveness of sins and the hope of everlasting life. They mocked Him, beat Him, ridiculed Him, lied about Him, and ultimately, killed Him. They intended to demean Him; instead, God used Jesus' submissive humility to save the world. In that moment, the judicial and righteous edict of condemnation for the human race was superseded by a new edict, a new covenant: the Good News of salvation, love, and hope. Paul described this transformational news in his letter to the Colossians: "When you were dead in your sins and in the uncircumcision of your sinful nature, God made you alive with Christ. He forgave us all our sins, having canceled the written code, with its regulations, that was against us and that stood opposed to us; he took it away, nailing it to the cross. And having disarmed the powers and authorities, he made a public spectacle of them, triumphing over them by the cross" (2:13–15 NIV 1984). By humility, sacrifice, and death, Jesus defeated the evil powers, conquered sin and death, and gave us new life. That's the paradoxical new edict posted on the cross that awful and glorious day!

Fifteen centuries ago, Saint Augustine marveled at the willing sacrifice of Jesus. He put it this way:

> Man's maker was made man that He, Ruler of the stars, might nurse at His mother's breast; that the Bread might hunger, the Fountain thirst, the Light sleep, the Way be tired on His journey; that Truth might be accused by false witnesses, the Teacher be beaten with whips, the Foundation be suspended on wood; that Strength might grow weak; that the Healer might be wounded; that Life might die.[7]

When we fully recognize Jesus' sacrifice, our hearts are melted and moved. We don't have to *try* to be passionate about God. Our devotion to Him is simply *a response* to His amazing love. Soon, we want more of what He wants, we value what He values, and we long to serve as He served.

Don't miss out on all the blessings God has for you. He has far more for you than you can imagine. Draw nearer to Jesus. Let His grace sink deep into your heart. Allow your heart to respond to His unconditional love. Act on His guidance, even if it means you have to make sacrifices. This is what being all-in requires. Keep your eyes focused on Jesus so your devotion doesn't fade. As we walk with Him, we'll go over mountains and through valleys, but we can be sure that He's with us all along the way.

Sometimes I shudder when I think of what would have happened if I hadn't responded to the Spirit of God that day in the recording studio. Before that day, I was miserable. I'd lost my peace. If I had never said yes to God, I would still be miserable and confused today. I would have missed out on the incomparable blessings God had in store for me, and I would have missed the sheer joy of seeing God use me to touch people's lives. Has it been worth it? Yes! It has been well worth it.

The promise of God is that the prize always outweighs the price. Count on it. Give yourself fully to Him. You'll never regret it.

> If you are not willing to risk the usual, you will have to settle for the ordinary.
>
> —JIM ROHN

A NOTE ABOUT THIS BOOK: At the end of each chapter, you'll find some reflection and discussion questions. Take time to think, pray, and write your responses. If you are in a class or a small group, use these questions to stimulate rich conversations. You'll learn a lot from one another.

CONSIDER THESE QUESTIONS

1. How would you describe what it means to be "all-in" with God? Is this attractive to you? Why or why not?
2. What difference does it make to see every job as God's calling to serve Him and represent Him to those around us?
3. What is your divine calling? How has God used (or how could He use) His Word, His Spirit, and His people to affirm your calling?

4. Read 1 Corinthians 2:9–10. How would it change your thinking and your actions if you really believed God has far more blessings for you than you can imagine?
5. Do you agree or disagree with the idea that most of us need to experience heartache, failure, and loss before we turn our eyes to God and seek Him above all else? Explain your answer.
6. What are some common excuses people use to bail out on making God their first priority and passion? Which of these have you used?
7. What's the difference between trying to muster up enough passion for God and letting the amazing reality of Christ's sacrifice melt and move your heart?

TWO

BLINDED BY SIGHT

Most people have a desire to look
for the exception instead of the
desire to become exceptional.

—JOHN C. MAXWELL

BEFORE CARLA AND I HAD CHILDREN, CHRISTMAS WAS A MAJOR THEATRICAL production in our home. She planned, shopped, and crafted all kinds of things to make it special. (We even had matching Christmas pajamas—but don't think about that too long!) For years, we had Christmas with our families in Arkansas. But during our first year in Chicago, we didn't have enough money to make the trip. We stayed in our little apartment in the city. That same year, a blizzard shut down the entire city. It was quite a shock for two people from the South!

We were far from home, but we still wanted to enjoy the family traditions we had grown to love. One of the most memorable traditions was helping my father make his cornbread dressing to accompany the smoked turkey. When he and I were on task, we pulled out all the stops and really enjoyed the process together. My grandma Faye had taught me how to make candied yams, so that became my holiday signature dish. (Yes, I eventually learned to cook more than sweet rice!) Now that Carla and I were alone this particular year, we took on the whole menu. I cooked candied yams, and Carla made black-eyed peas (and plenty of other things) for a colossal banquet for two. To follow in my father's footsteps, I made the dressing.

The day before Christmas, I had called my dad to ask him for the recipe. He said, "The first thing is that you have to make your own cornbread."

I was writing everything down, but I interrupted him, "So . . . that mix will work, won't it?"

There was a long pause, then he said, "No, son. You don't use a mix. You make it from scratch!"

He went through all the ingredients, the mixing process, the cooking temperature, and how long to bake it. He told me what to look for on the edges of the dressing when it needed to come out of the oven. When he finished, he informed me, "Son, most people put sage in their dressing, but I don't. If you want to, you can."

I thanked him and made a list of what I needed to buy at the store. Just to be sure I got everything right, I went on the Internet to look at some other recipes for dressing. Almost all of them included sage. I decided I'd put sage in my recipe since "most people" use it.

After I got back from the store, I rolled up my sleeves and went to work. I cooked a panful of cornbread, crumbled it up, and then mixed the remaining ingredients in a bowl. It looked and smelled just like my dad's recipe. Then I said to myself, *Great. Now it's time for the sage.* My grandmother never measured anything, but I thought I'd put about three very generous tablespoons of sage into my small, glass mixing bowl.

I spread the dressing mixture out in a pan and put it in the oven. At the appointed time, I took it out. It looked perfect; I couldn't wait to try it. I stuck my fork in and pulled out a big bite. With eager anticipation, I put it in my mouth. *Uggghhh!* It was horrible! It was the nastiest stuff I had ever tasted. I was spitting and coughing, and my mouth was on fire.

Carla came running in. "What's going on? What's wrong with you?"

I pointed my fork at the beautiful, steaming pan of dressing and said, "Don't eat it. It's poison!"

I soon discovered the problem: the recipe that called for three tablespoons of sage was for enough dressing to feed a small army. I was only making dressing for two people—Carla and me. Except for one ingredient, my dressing was fit for a king. I could have taken a picture of it and put it in any cookbook. But I wouldn't even feed it to my dog. One ingredient in the wrong amount ruined the whole dish. It's the same for you and me in our relationship with God. We can have everything in place and working correctly, but the incorrect use of a single element can lead to disaster.

In the lives of countless Christians, that one element is their self-image. When it's based on anything but the love and grace of God, it becomes flawed, shaky, and potentially poisonous (to our souls). We may have all the outward appearance of being spiritually healthy, but inside, we're insecure.

I'm not suggesting that people have to follow a single recipe in their relationship with God. Just as there are hundreds of good recipes for dressing, we can find plenty of different models of vibrant spiritual life. Baptists, Methodists, Charismatics, Lutherans, and Presbyterians worship, pray, and serve in different ways, but they can't be spiritually healthy if they don't have one specific ingredient: the belief that the grace of Jesus Christ is their only source of security, hope, delight, and purpose. Nothing else will do, though we try everything else we can think of!

TWO MIRRORS

When people walk down the street, most of them instinctively look at their reflections in the windows. It's a knee-jerk reaction. I believe there are two mirrors in each of our lives. One reflects the world's values; the other reflects God's truth about us. Far too often, we're gazing into the wrong mirror. We've drawn conclusions—about ourselves, about God, and about our purpose in life—based on faulty, distorted information.

The world's mirror is similar to a carnival mirror, reflecting distortions and untruths to whomever stands before it. We can appear tall and skinny (We like that one!), or we can appear short and fat. Another one can reflect our images in ripples, like a potato chip. Though we laugh at each other and ourselves in these carnival moments, having a distorted self-image is serious business—it ruins our motivation, steals our joy, and warps our relationships.

The mirrors we see each day scream that success, pleasure, approval, physical appearance, intelligence, and our "cool factor" or "swag" determine who we are and how high we can go. These metaphorical measuring sticks can't possibly result in strength, stability, hope, or security. Instead, they produce either shame or pride. When we think we're doing better than the person next to us, we feel superior. We've arrived! But when we realize the other person is smarter, richer, better looking, and has more friends, we feel like a failure. Some of us habitually stay in one condition or the other, but most of us vacillate from pride to shame, then back again, several times a day.

Advertisers have gone to great lengths to create powerful verbal and visual concoctions of dissatisfaction and hope. Dissatisfaction with who we are and what we have comes first. Then, we hope the product or service will make us happy, successful, and popular. For instance, women long to look like the models in magazines, but we all know these models have been airbrushed and digitally altered to make them artificially gorgeous. Nobody actually looks like that! I've even had graphic designers Photoshop my pictures for album covers and promotional pieces to make me look taller, thinner, or younger. One of the pictures was altered so much, I looked like a teenage boy! I told the designers to go with the real, middle-aged me. A study of models revealed that the most envied women on the planet often suffer from depression, anorexia, bulimia, loneliness, and other problems of a devastated self-conception.

We constantly compare ourselves to others. As a result, we spend too much time, money, and energy trying to manage our image. We wear "masks" to impress people because we're terrified others will see the real person underneath. We don't want anyone to know how fearful and insecure we are. Eventually, we may not even recognize our true selves. We are constantly seeking our authenticity, but our flawed sight blinds us.

Even the heights of beauty, fame, and wealth can't fill the void of an empty heart. We all know people who appear to be beating the system. They might be music moguls, business tycoons, head-turning beauties, or brilliant scholars. Everyone looks at them and marvels. Even these people, though, realize they aren't what they project to the outside world. In a famous *Vanity Fair* article, Madonna confessed that every new song she released made her feel alive, but in between, she felt lost and alone. She told the reporter, "My drive in life is from this horrible fear of being mediocre. And that's always pushing me, pushing me. Because even though I've become Somebody, I still have to prove that Somebody. My struggle has never ended and it probably never will."[1]

Chris Evert, the professional tennis star, admitted that she struggled with her sense of inadequacy and used victories on the court as a salve. She said:

> I had no idea who I was, or what I could be away from tennis. I was depressed and afraid because so much of my life had been defined by my being a tennis champion. I was completely lost. Winning made me feel like I was somebody. It made me feel pretty. It was like being hooked on a drug. I needed the wins, the applause, in order to have an identity.[2]

If we live to impress the people around us, it would be easy to conclude that God would be our harshest critic. If we need to wear a mask around anyone, we might think we need to hide ourselves from God! That's what Adam and Eve did when they sinned in the Garden and wore fig leaves to hide their nakedness. The paradox of the Christian faith is that God knows every detail about us, even our deepest thoughts, and He loves us still. We can't hide from Him—a paradoxical fact that can be deeply comforting yet terribly threatening.

King David knew both sides of the omniscience of God: He knows everything about us. David wrote:

> O Lord, you have searched me and you know me. You know when I sit and when I rise; you perceive my thoughts from afar. You discern my going out and my lying down; you are familiar with all my ways. Before a word is on my tongue you know it completely, O Lord. (Ps. 139:1–4 NIV 1984)

Does God know our hidden feelings? Yes. Does He know our selfish thoughts? Certainly. Does He know our deepest and most sinister desires? Of course. God knows it all. Nothing is hidden from His sight. But He is quick to forgive and abounds in love for us. He doesn't wink at our sin. He forgives it. He doesn't make excuses for our selfishness. He sent Jesus to pay the price for it. In an article in *Christianity Today,* Mark Galli explained, "The very thing that makes us feel trapped—God's omniscience—is the very thing that reveals the depth of God's grace. If we can muster the courage to allow God's omniscience to judge us, we will see that before and after the righteous judgment, there has been the omniscience of grace."[3]

Because of grace, we can be fully, totally, and completely honest with God about every sin in our lives. The cross is the promise that God won't condemn us. If we had to earn God's approval, we'd be in deep trouble because we can't meet His standard of holiness. But Jesus did, and Jesus does. When we receive the forgiveness offered in the sacrifice of Christ's death on the cross, God puts all our sin on Jesus and puts all of His righteousness on us. It's the greatest exchange of grace in the history of the universe!

HEIRS AND COHEIRS

When an older relative dies, we sometimes expect to receive an inheritance. It could be a piece of costume jewelry, or it could be a million dollars. It depends on the wealth and generosity of our relative. Spiritually, we have an older relative. Jesus is older than time itself! John tells us that Jesus "was with God" and "was God" (John 1:1). He is the Ancient of Days. He existed from eternity past, and since He's outside time, He already exists in eternity future. That's mind-bending to try and comprehend! Jesus doesn't just own some pieces of old jewelry or a stack of money; He reigns throughout the universe! Paul made the stunning statement that when Jesus died, we, God's children, became the Father's heirs and coheirs with Jesus. He explained this to the Christians in Rome: "Now if we are children, then we are heirs—heirs of God and coheirs with Christ, if indeed we share in his sufferings in order that we may also share in his glory" (Rom. 8:17). Jesus identified with us on the cross so He could pay for our sins. Then He put us in the family of God so we could be coheirs with Him. What do we inherit? The entire, amazing wealth of heaven: forgiveness, adoption, power, purpose, and glory. And because we are identified with Him, we can also expect to share in His suffering—not death to pay for anyone's sins, but gladly sacrificing our comfort to introduce the world to the Savior. This—and nothing less—is the vast expanse of God's grace to you and me!

The astounding truth in the Bible is that God doesn't just tolerate us or shake His head and wonder what to do with us. The Father loves us just as much as He loves His own Son, Jesus. On the night before Jesus was betrayed, He spent time with His disciples to teach them more about the Spirit and the kingdom. He also prayed for them and for us. At the end of the prayer, He said, "I have made you known to them, and will continue to make you known in order that the love you have for me may be in them and that I myself may be in them" (John 17:26). Do you see it? The love the Father has for Jesus is the exact same love He has for you and me! No difference. If God merely tolerated us, we wouldn't be amazed at His grace. If we had to measure up by earning enough points to avoid His anger, we would not fall at His feet in wonder and affection. Our security, identity, and motivation are rooted in something far more precious—the fact that almighty God adores us and calls us His own. Let me put it this way: if our hearts don't sing and our minds don't marvel at God's great love for us, we haven't grasped it yet. That love is the foundation of a good and godly self-conception.

In our relationship with God, some of us see ourselves as consumers, some as employees, and some as beloved children. Some people see God as a celestial Santa Claus who should give them whatever they want. When their expectations aren't met (and a loving Father always has bigger purposes than fulfilling every desire), they pout and claim He doesn't love them. Many people have a very different but equally destructive view of God: as an associate in a business relationship. They believe they've negotiated a contract: they'll do their part, and God had better do His—which is to bless them and make their lives easy and financially prosperous. Again, God has bigger, higher, and deeper goals for His children. He wants to bless each of us, but He delights in blessing those who are humble and thankful, not those who are demanding. (In that way, He's no different from all other parents!) Those who see God as a loving, wise Father thank Him for His blessings and trust Him when they don't understand what He's up to. He gives each of us, as His children, a role in the family business—reclaiming lost souls and restoring God's glory to the earth. God wants to convince us that He's that kind of Father so we can respond as His loving, grateful, obedient children.

No matter what we've done or who we were, we're no longer the same when we put our lives into the hand of God. In Christ, we're new creations. The old has passed away, and the new has come (2 Cor. 5:17). God isn't keeping a secret list of our sins and waiting to use them to crush us. In Christ, there is no condemnation. All our sins—past, present, and future—have been washed away in the tidal wave of Jesus' cleansing blood. Yes, we still struggle with sin and temptation. We're still flawed people in a fallen world, but we have a new identity as chosen, beloved, forgiven children of the King! There will be a day when we no longer experience sin and death, but not yet. That day is coming, and we look forward to it. It will be our ultimate inheritance. What we have now is a down payment on that future glory. For now, we still have to fight the good fight and finish the race God has given us to run. If our self-conception is based on our talents, appearance, or intelligence, we'll always struggle with shame and pride. But if our identity is firmly rooted in the rich soil of God's grace, we'll draw on His infinite resources of love and power, and we'll stay strong.

Feelings of inadequacy blind us to the possibilities of what it would look like to take the lid off our lives and live all-in for God. When we're worried about our past, we can't walk with confidence into the future, and we encounter many disastrous attempts along the way. Likewise, to drive while looking in the rearview mirror almost guarantees a wreck! Future-forward living provides a safety net and opens us up to God's messages. But some of us feel so bad about our past that we have no hope for the future. We fail to realize God has wiped the past clean! Others want to go back to the relationships and the experiences they once enjoyed. They're so preoccupied with the past that they cannot envision a more hopeful future. Still others are trying to make up for past failures. To some extent, this is good and noble and right. Repentance involves restitution to repay those who suffered loss from our poor choices. But some of these people aren't making restitution. They're trying to show the world that they've really got it, they've made it, and no one is going to hold them down ever again. Sadly, that's a form of twisted pride, not humble repentance.

When managing our image is our main goal in life, we miss out on God's purpose for us. We don't focus on pleasing God, but on impressing people. We change our values and behaviors to fit in with those we're around at the moment. We spend excessive amounts of money to impress others, we attend certain events to raise our social standing, and we do things hoping to gain the acceptance of others. This way of living is not about God at all. It's about fitting in. When we get a smile or a laugh from someone, we feel great. When we receive a frown or are ignored, we feel humiliation. We then try to do anything to win back that person's approval.

We need to remind ourselves that *people* didn't create us. *God* did. People don't offer us eternal life. God does. People don't have the power of the universe in their hands; God does. People don't have a plan for us that's both challenging and thrilling—and makes us partners with the King of all. God does.

GOD'S CREATION

You're the creative brilliance of God Himself. You are not junk. In the same psalm that David wrote about God's omniscience, he described how God beautifully and uniquely crafted each of us. David wrote:

> For you created my inmost being; you knit me together in my mother's womb. I praise you because I am fearfully and wonderfully made; your works are wonderful, I know that full well. My frame was not hidden from you when I was made in the secret place, when I was woven together in the depths of the earth. Your eyes saw my unformed body; all the days ordained for me were written in your book before one of them came to be. How precious to me are your thoughts, God! How vast is the sum of them! (Ps. 139:13–17)

God knows everything about us, but this knowledge isn't recent. He was there when we were formed in our mothers' wombs. He knows our personalities and our potential. He knows our character flaws and our greatest talents. We can't fool God. He knows the very worst about us, but He loves us with tender mercy. He's not holding our past against us. Instead, He offers us a fantastic future. He knows how badly we've failed, but He declares that we have unlimited potential. He's not holding the lid on our lives; we are. He's cheering for us to take the lid off! He wants us to prosper. His vision for us is far higher and greater than our own. He's not holding us back. He declares us to be victorious!

When I preached on this passage in church one Sunday, I told the congregation to turn to one another and say, "I am marvelous!" But I told them to say it like this: "I am mahhh-velous!" It's not just a sentence; it's a declaration of our identity in Jesus Christ. In Him, we *are* marvelous!

PRECIOUS THOUGHTS

One of the statements in David's prayer is his shout of joy: "How precious to me are your thoughts, God!" Can we say that too? Absolutely! Many of us assume God's thoughts toward us are angry, condemning, and dismissive. Maybe we formed this opinion from a parent who was harsh or who abandoned us. Perhaps this conception of God came from a preacher who yelled more about God's condemnation than spoke lovingly of His grace. It's possible we are far more aware of the darkness of our sins than the brilliant light of Christ's forgiveness. Whatever the reason, many of us—I'm including sincere Christians who are regularly in church and who serve faithfully—believe God frowns at us instead of smiling as a loving, proud Father.

God's thoughts about you and me are precious to us because they are full of grace and truth. Yes, He knows the worst about us, but He loves us with unshakable affection. When Jesus was baptized, God's voice rang out over the Jordan River: "This is my Son, whom I love; with him I am well pleased" (Matt. 3:17). This proclamation of love and delight was spoken before Jesus did anything. It wasn't an evaluation of performance; it was esteem for a person. In the same way, when we place our faith in Jesus Christ and are born again into God's family, God says the same thing about us: "This is my son, my daughter, whom I love, with him or her I am well pleased." Do you feel that love deep in your bones? It's the source of genuine security and a foundation for a life of courage, faith, and adventure.

Christians begin as spiritual infants and grow to spiritual maturity—at least, we're supposed to grow that way. As we grow in the knowledge of God, He imparts a sense of direction, wisdom, and purpose into our souls. Gradually, we realize we were made for more than acquiring earthly stuff and impressing people. We were created to make a significant difference. Many passages of Scripture tell us that we have the privilege of joining God in reclaiming the human race for His glory. One of my favorite passages in the Bible is God's statement recorded by the prophet Jeremiah. The people in his day had been devastated by war, famine, and exile. (And we think we have it bad!) Even in their calamity, God gave them a strong hope:

> "For I know the plans I have for you," declares the Lord, "plans to prosper you and not to harm you, plans to give you hope and a future. Then you will call on me and come and pray to me, and I will listen to you. You will seek me and find me when you seek

> me with all your heart.'" (Jer. 29:11–13)

I have to be honest. It only takes one negative statement from anyone to ruin my day. I once preached a sermon called "Being a Low-Class Church." I knew the title would confuse some people, so I explained that Jesus had stepped out of heaven to become one of us. He had been high class (one with God in heaven), but He became low class to reach out and touch us. We don't want to be a prideful church whose members look down on those less fortunate. I taught that God wants us to follow Jesus' example and reach out to the misfits, the outcasts, the poor, the immigrants, the struggling moms, and the distant dads—the least, the lost, the last, and the left out. These are "the least of these," whom Jesus loves (see Matt. 25:31–40). If we love Him, we'll love those whom society casts out too. God's grace brings all of us into the upper class of His kingdom. I reminded the congregation of Peter's words about all of God's children:

> But you are a chosen people, a royal priesthood, a holy nation, God's special possession, that you may declare the praises of him who called you out of darkness into his wonderful light. Once you were not a people, but now you are the people of God; once you had not received mercy, but now you have received mercy. (1 Peter 2:9–10)

I explained that it's not enough to feel sorry for those less-fortunate people. We first have to genuinely care *about* them and then actively care *for* them. It takes the experience of God's love and power to do that. I wanted to be very practical. If a homeless person who smells off-putting were to sit near them, they shouldn't refuse to shake his hand (or get up and move to a seat on the other side of the church). God's people need to reach out and touch him and acknowledge his presence, free from judgment.

One Sunday at our church, a prostitute had the courage to walk in and sit among us. Everybody accurately assumed her profession, mainly by the way she dressed but also by the fact that she allowed me to identify her in church. She felt she should and could be in that church seat. And she was right! Jesus was known as "a friend of sinners" (Matt. 11:19; Luke 7:34). How are we known? Do the outcasts in our community know us as their friends or as their self-righteous critics? I concluded the sermon that day, saying, "Jesus emptied Himself to come to us. He became low class, and we need to be like Him in becoming a low-class church." I asked the congregation to write the names of some outcasts on cards. If they didn't know the names, they could just describe those individuals. Next, I asked them to make a commitment to reach out to these people in very specific, tangible, warm, welcoming ways during the week.

When I finished my message, I could tell I had hit a nerve. Some members even had a look on their faces that told me the Spirit had spoken directly to their hearts that morning. The majority were convicted and convinced, ready to take steps of faith. I got a lot of notes and phone calls from people who told me how God had used my message in their lives.

It was an incredible service. People felt empowered. Our ambassadors (volunteers) were excited to join God and one another in reaching every person in our community, and more people than ever volunteered to serve. It was wonderful!

Then I got another response. Before the next week's service, a lady came up to me and said, "Pastor, I need to talk to you about last week's sermon."

The look on her face told me her response wasn't heartfelt

conviction and repentance. She was going to correct me! I answered, "Yes, ma'am. What would you like to say about it?"

She glared at me and angrily said, "I didn't like it. Not one bit."

I waited for her to explain, but she didn't continue. I pressed for information. "I understand, but why didn't you like it?"

"We shouldn't be a low-class church!" Her implication was that she wasn't going to tolerate us being a low-class people.

I tried to explain. "Maybe you didn't understand the context of the term. I wasn't saying that our church isn't committed to excellence. The point of the message was that we need to use the resources God has given us to reach out to all of those He loves—including those our *society* considers to be low class."

Man, I wished I'd said it that clearly the previous Sunday! Surely I'd convinced her that we were committed to following the example of Jesus.

She just shook her head and said, "No, you're missing it, Pastor."

I gently told her, "I'm sorry you're offended by what I said last week, but it's the Word of the Lord. You'll have to take it up with Him."

My words sounded as if I were completely assured and strong, but her criticism cut me like a knife. It was just one comment—from a person who didn't understand the basic concept of my message—and I'd gotten hundreds of positive messages during the week. Yet her voice drowned out all the rest. For weeks, her voice resonated in the back of my mind every time I prepared my sermons, every time I spoke, every time I led a meeting, and even in the quiet, private moments when I was thinking and praying. I worried about the perception of this one woman. Soon, I began to wonder if others felt as she did but hadn't said anything to me. Her criticism became more important than the conviction and confidence of the Holy Spirit in my life. I was letting a thirty-second conversation cloud my mind and rob me of joy.

Weeks later, I finally learned an important lesson. The absurdity hit me, and I thought, *What am I doing?* I stepped back and realized that I had been giving a lone, critical voice far more power than it deserved. It wasn't that I should heap scorn on this woman (or anyone else who questions or criticizes me). I needed to love her as Jesus loved His detractors, but I didn't need to give her (or anyone) the keys to my heart! If I lose my focus on God's evaluation of me based on His grace and love, a single critical comment or note can destroy my self-confidence.

I don't think I'm the only one who wrestles with negative messages. Teenagers are vulnerable to the taunts of friends. Spouses long for intimacy, but they constantly risk being hurt by words of comparison or condemnation. At work, bosses know how to push our buttons and keep us off balance by using mixed messages of praise and criticism. At church, a lady might wonder what other women think of her dress, or a man might wonder if anyone will ignore him or make fun of him based on his profession. In every meaningful relationship, we hear important statements about our worth. Too often, we don't filter them. Our goal should be to discard the negative and embrace the positive. Too often, we get our identity and self-image from the lips of people instead of the heart of God.

We can't stop people from speaking negative messages into our lives—and we need to listen to them to see if they're true so we can learn from them—but we don't have to give those messages more power than the affirming, positive, soul-satisfying messages of the love of God. I need to constantly give God's thoughts more value than anyone else's. His thoughts, His evaluation, and His words of hope and challenge need to be riveted to the center of my heart. His messages are precious. The negative messages I hear from people or the evil one are noise I need to tune out.

The Enemy of our souls uses our insecurity and negative messages to rob us of our full potential and convince us that we can never take the lid off. As long as we feel inferior, "less than," and desperate to please those around us, we can't fully experience the joy and power God has for us. God has plans to prosper us, but we fail to see His plans if we become consumed with hopes of measuring up to people's expectations and fears that we'll never please them. Distraction is one of the most effective tools of the Enemy, and many of us fall for it over and over again. When we're distracted, we don't even give a thought to God's purpose, we don't seek His blessing, and we miss out on His favor.

The struggle with self-conception isn't limited to a few people. It's a universal problem. We live in a world that shouts that we can't measure up until and unless we meet someone else's expectations and achieve a certain standard of beauty, wealth, and power. And beyond the world's pervasive messages, human nature is insecure. Even those who have "made it" in the world's eyes intuitively know they don't measure up. (Remember the statements from Madonna and Chris Evert that I quoted earlier?) God has made us so that only He can fill the deepest void in our hearts and give us our highest meaning. He is the source of our true identity. This identity is based on the solid rock of His grace and gives us more joy and challenge than anything else life can offer.

We need to understand that God didn't come up with His divine plans for us this morning. David reminds us, "When I was woven together in the depths of the earth[,] [y]our eyes saw my unformed body" (Ps. 139:15–16). God constructed His purpose for us before the foundations of the earth were established, before we were born, and before we were born again. God saw our potential and began crafting us before the world began! He creates us with the right parents, in the right culture, at the right time, under the right circumstances. The reality to which we are each born is not always ideal to us as humans, but it is the best one because God chose those circumstances in order to best shape us, prepare us, and give us opportunities to shine. In God's grand plans for us, He knew He would forgive us, adopt us, empower us with His Spirit, place us in a network of relationships, equip us with talents and gifts, and lead us to find our true purpose. We may wander off track for a while, but God graciously uses even our stumbles to teach us lessons we need to accomplish His will. God doesn't waste our sins, and He doesn't waste our pain. If we'll let Him, He'll weave everything together into a tapestry of beauty and blessing for us and for the benefit of others.

Earlier in his life, my friend Chris seemed to many to be a lost cause. He was so far away from God that many people thought he would never amount to anything. He ran away from God and from his family. He got heavily into drinking, and his life spiraled out of control. His mother wondered why in the world God had given her such a son.

But God saw something even his mother could not see. Chris remembers his mother complaining, "Lord, what kind of child did You give me? He's a drunkard, and throwing up from his indulgences. He is hopeless. This has got to be a mistake!" But God loved Chris and saw his unlimited potential.

Chris told me, "I'm so glad that God didn't look at me through my mother's eyes. She was blind to my worth and my potential, but God infused His grace into me, raised me up, and gave me a place in His kingdom." Now Chris is a very gifted pastor, teacher, father, and friend who is being used incredibly by the hand of God.

Some people believe they're lost causes. Many have been abused or abandoned. Some are trying to make it as single parents. The world—and even our mothers—may have concluded that we're helpless, hopeless, and worthless. But God has a very different estimation. God isn't looking at us through the eyes of our parents, our friends, our enemies, or the ads we see each day. He's looking at us through His eyes of tender love, profound hope, and strong confidence that we can become all He intends for us to be—when we take the lid off.

All of us assume what we see in the mirror is the absolute truth. In fact, most of us are blinded by our sight. What we see is only a distortion of God's love and a distraction from God's best. We need to look in the lovely, powerful mirror of God's truth and learn to see ourselves the way God sees us. When we get a glimpse of our new identity in Jesus Christ, no one can stop us from taking the lid off!

> We should be astonished at the goodness of God, stunned that He should bother to call us by name, our mouths wide open at His love, bewildered that at this very moment we are standing on holy ground.
>
> —BRENNAN MANNING

CONSIDER THESE QUESTIONS

1. How would you define and describe the two mirrors we look into each day? What are the impacts of each one?
2. Think about your favorite ads. What is the surface promise of the product or service? What is the underlying promise of meaning, power, popularity, and

comfort?

3. Does God's omniscience terrify you or comfort you? Explain your answer.
4. What's the difference between marveling at God's love and acceptance and thinking we have to jump through enough hoops to avoid His anger and earn His blessings? How does a healthy grasp of God's grace shape our self-image, our security, and our motivation to take the lid off in our lives?
5. Read 1 Peter 2:9–10. How does Peter describe your identity? What difference would it make to see yourself this way?
6. Before you read this chapter, how did you imagine God's view of you? How about now?
7. How would it affect your joy, your commitment, and your destiny if you fully grasped your new identity in Christ?

PART 2

OUTWARD

THREE

UPSIDE DOWN

In the Garden, mankind shifted from acceptance, grace, and love to blame, shame, and the compulsion to prove ourselves by our performance. To recapture God's design, we need new voices that penetrate our crusty defenses and speak to our souls, not only inspiring our actions, but even more, enflaming our hearts.

—SAMUEL R. CHAND

WHEN I WAS BEGINNING THE NINTH GRADE, OUR FAMILY HAD JUST MOVED TO Arkansas, where my dad was assigned to pastor a Methodist church. Soon after we arrived and moved in, the Reids, a prominent family in the church, invited us over to their house for dinner. That's the custom in the South.

My brothers and I sat at the kids' table, but I was more interested in the adults' conversation than in the children's banter. As dessert was served, I moved my chair closer to hear Mr. Reid tell stories. He told one that I've never forgotten. He said that in Arkansas, autumn can sneak up with a cold spell after the warmth of an "Indian summer." Years ago, he explained, a cold front unexpectedly blew through. It surprised the people, and it shocked the animals. A man walked out in his driveway and found a snake that hadn't made it to the warm shelter of its hole. The snake appeared frozen, but the man thought it still might be alive. He felt sorry for the poor little critter. He picked it up and put it in his coat pocket so the warmth of his body could revive it.

About an hour later, the man felt a searing pain in his side. He opened his coat and saw that the snake had, in fact, revived, and it had bitten him! The man was stunned. He spoke to the snake, "What do you think you're doing? I picked you up, tenderly cared for you, and gave you a safe, warm place to revive you—and you bit me! What kind of thanks is that?"

The snake looked at the man and flatly replied, "Well, you knew I was a snake when you picked me up."

Mr. Reid was making a point as old as the Garden and as new as today's culture. The snake is the world's system of values, and we are the naive man who holds it close without thinking of the probable consequences. The world promises ultimate meaning if we pursue personal power, success, affluence, and outward beauty (vanity). Everywhere we turn, these promises ring in our ears . . . and they resonate in our hearts. We pick them up, fondle them, and caress them—and we're shocked when they bite us!

They bite us in many different ways. They *distract* us by taking our attention away from God's mercy, justice, and glory. They *disillusion* us, because no matter how much control, fame, wealth, and attractiveness we obtain, someone else always has a little bit more. And ultimately, they *destroy* us, because they suck the life out of us. We're like the rat on the treadmill, running faster and faster but getting nowhere. We acquire more stuff and power, but it doesn't satisfy, so we try to acquire even more. Sooner or later, we're exhausted, and we've ruined our most important relationships. We become empty shells of what God has intended us to be. The world's empty promises are a ten-ton lid on God's magnificent design for us! To take the lid off, we have to realize God's kingdom and values are exactly upside down from the world's values.

The answer isn't to become hermits. The solution is to recognize that we are *in* the world, but we aren't *of* the world (John 17:13–19). We're citizens of heaven (Phil. 3:20), delivered from the domain of darkness and transferred into the kingdom of God (Col. 1:13–14)—not just when we die, but now. We have dual citizenship: we're Americans (or Canadians or Romanians or whatever), but our first allegiance is to a different realm and to its King.

TWO WAYS TO SEE THE WORLD'S TEMPTATIONS

The world's grip on most people is incredibly strong and equally deceptive. Two terms give us an insight into the power of the world's promises: *slavery* and *addiction*. Slaves are under the domination of their master. They do what their master commands and go where he says to go. Slaves may despise their condition, but they often have given up on ever being free. They tend to accept their place, their poverty, and their destiny. In the same way, many people are slaves of the lure to get more. All day every day, their minds are consumed by the demands to get more possessions and increase their popularity and power. In fact, they can't imagine living any other way!

The second analogy is that our attraction to the world's values is addictive. Some addictions are chemical (alcohol, cocaine, heroin, meth, nicotine), while others are essentially behavioral (gambling, sex, shopping, food). Both forms of addiction alter the basic chemistry of the brain. It's easy to understand that inserting foreign substances into our brains changes them, but recurring, destructive behaviors have a similar impact. In *Unchain Your Brain*,[1] Dr. Daniel Amen explained that both forms of addiction create an imbalance of two chemicals necessary for our brains to function normally: serotonin and dopamine. Psychiatrists and psychologists recognize a compulsive cycle in any addiction.

- Searching

  First, people feel empty and needy, so they look for their substance or behavior of choice. They are convinced it will fill the hole in their hearts, numb the pain, and give them at least a short time of pleasure.
- Attraction

  When people find what they're looking for, their eyes light up with attraction. Shoppers see the dress or fishing rod they've wanted. Alcoholics pay for the bottle. We can almost taste the pleasure we'll get from being appreciated by a boss, from dominating our spouses and kids, from winning an award, or from enjoying relief of any kind.
- Relief

  When we experience the thing we've longed for, we often feel thrilled—even euphoric. For a moment, it seems to give us everything we wanted, but the feeling doesn't last long.
- Anxiety

  When the thrill wears off, we begin to feel nervous. The emptiness returns, and we end up feeling more anxious than ever. We become desperate to fill the hole with something—anything!—that promises joy and relief again.
- Denial and desperation

  Most of us can't stand the constant awareness that our pursuits are empty, so we lie. We lie to ourselves, to our families, and to our friends. We claim the addictive behavior is really giving us all we hoped it would give. We may even convince ourselves that our desperate feelings aren't really true, so we begin the search phase again.

- Withdrawal

  As anxiety, denial, and desperation take their toll, the person disengages from people, especially those who have a clear perception about the addictive behavior. The intense feelings of loneliness and helplessness trigger the next search phase, and the cycle begins again.

During all of this, our brains are working overtime. The chemicals are out of balance, demanding relief and promising fulfillment. The behavior or substance fulfills the promise for a moment, but the destructive pattern soon continues.

Another feature of an addiction is tolerance: over time, we need more of the drug or behavior to give us the same kind of high. The amount that gave us pleasure yesterday just doesn't cut it today. We seek out more potent substances or behaviors—more alcohol, more powerful weed, higher career prestige, a bigger car, a nicer house, and a more lavish vacation. Yesterday's thrills leave us flat.

As you've been reading about these phases, you've probably thought of people you love who are trapped in this cycle of addiction. But ask yourself, are you trapped in it too? Are you hooked on the promise of control, power, affirmation, and pleasure? These pursuits cause very significant changes in brain chemistry, and they are genuinely addictive. For most of us, our addictions aren't as obvious because most everyone has an addiction to something. Some addictions are just more socially acceptable than others.

The promise of God is a kind of reverse slavery and addiction. The more we love and follow God, the more we will experience true freedom instead of oppression. When God's love and blessings flow into our lives, we are always fulfilled, unlike our response to addictions, which leave us empty and craving. When our lid is off, strange and wonderful things happen: our selfish desires take a backseat, and we desire to be channels of blessing to others. Instead of living only for our pleasure, our power, and our possessions, we want to see God work His miracles in the lives of those around us. When we see God using us in this way, we feel euphoric, but it produces gratitude and humility instead of greed, fear, and pride. The way God affects us is the opposite from the way the world affects us. He instills peace and love instead of hopelessness and fear.

When we tap into the grace of Jesus Christ, we experience the full riches of His love and power. We sense the abundance of His great love, and we know it's not going to be taken away. He is immutable and unchangeable—the same yesterday, today, and forever. Nothing can separate us from the love of God found in Jesus. When we rest in that assurance, we have the courage to take the lid off and attempt great things for His glory and honor.

BACKWARD

Jesus didn't come to make good people a little better. He came to rescue helplessly lost people from sin, guilt, and death. He came to change their direction and destiny. In the same way, He didn't come to earth to suffer, die, and be raised from the tomb in order to give us a little help as we pursue the world's values. He came to radically reorient us to His values. One writer summarized the principles of His upside-down kingdom like this:

The way up is down.
The way to gain power is by serving selflessly.
The last shall be first and the first shall be last.
The way to true wealth is to give generously.
The outcasts and misfits are precious.
Only those who recognize they are weak can become truly strong.
The path to true life is to choose to die.[2]

The upside-down kingdom is central in the life and teaching of Jesus. He gave all to gain all. He humbled Himself but was exalted to the right hand of the Father. He died so that we might live. In a dramatic statement of this perspective, Jesus told His disciples:

> "If anyone would come after me, he must deny himself and take up his cross and follow me. For whoever wants to save his life will lose it, but whoever loses his life for me will find it. What good will it be for a man if he gains the whole world, yet forfeits his soul? Or what can a man give in exchange for his soul?" (Matt. 16:24–26 NIV 1984)

The upside-down kingdom operates in our lives today just as it operated in the life and times of Jesus. We can only live an all-in life if we first die to our old one. We gain true life by letting go of our demands to get what the world promises. In another mind-blowing statement in His most famous sermon, Jesus told the crowd that those who are truly blessed aren't the rich, the powerful, or the beautiful. Instead, those blessed are the humble and poor in spirit; the mourners; the ones who put others first; the ones who hunger and thirst for righteousness instead of personal gain; the ones who show mercy instead of intimidation; and the ones who have pure hearts, seek peace, and sacrifice personal comforts (Matt. 5:3–12). He was offering a truly radical, new way of living.

Jesus finished this sermon by pointing to two houses—one built on sand, and the other built on solid rock. Both houses experienced the same storm. Threats came from all sides: rains fell down, winds blew from the side, and water rose to batter the foundations. The house built on sandy soil represents those who may go to church, sing the songs, and carry their Bibles, but their hearts are still craving what the world offers. When storms come in their lives, they crumble into resentment, self-pity, and blame. The other house represents people who grasp the upside-down nature of God's kingdom. They realize every blessing comes from God's hand, and every difficulty is a chance to demonstrate God's grace and strength. When storms come, they aren't surprised or shattered. They may lose a few shingles and some paint, but their foundation stays strong.

OVERFLOW OF LIVING WATER

It's always been the default mode of the human heart to put the world's values on top, but the past few decades have accelerated the trend. Daniel Yankelovich, the author of *New Rules,* studied changes in the culture. He observed that in the 1950s, the country made a dramatic shift from self-sacrifice to self-indulgence. In other words, when we got over the suffering of the Great Depression and World War II, people became self-absorbed. They wanted all they could get because of their prior lack. Today, the trend toward self-indulgence is accelerating. Modern technology gives us incredible opportunities to communicate, but the subtle message underneath is that we should have everything we want whenever we want it.

The message of the gospel of Christ stands in bold opposition to this trend toward self-indulgence. But God doesn't shake His finger at us and *demand* that we change. He *invites* us to go with Him on the adventure of bringing a spiritual revolution to the hearts of people in the next bedroom, around our communities, and across the globe. When Jesus spoke to His disciples about giving their lives, He began, "If anyone would come after me . . ." That's a gracious offer, not harsh condemnation. He makes the same invitation to us today.

The upside-down kingdom begins with us, but it doesn't end with us. After we've taken the lid off by looking inward, we need to take it off again by looking outward. As we saw in the first two chapters, God has to work His grace and power into our lives first so that we have something to offer those around us. When our hearts are full, we naturally and instinctively want others to experience the fullness of God too. At a festival in Jerusalem, Jesus watched all the ceremonies for several days. There were sacrifices and washings, teaching and prayers. Each day's events were a little more important than the last. Finally, the time was right. John tells us:

> On the last and greatest day of the Feast, Jesus stood and said in a loud voice, "If anyone is thirsty, let him come to me and drink. Whoever believes in me, as the Scripture has said, streams of living water will flow from within him." By this he meant the Spirit, whom those who believed in him were later to receive. Up to that time the Spirit had not been given, since Jesus had not yet been glorified. (John 7:37–39 NIV 1984)

We don't manufacture the streams of living water that flow from us. We simply drink deeply of Jesus, and the springs flow. The water quenches our thirst, and as it flows out of us, it quenches the spiritual thirst of others who are parched and dry. Jesus explained that this new power and new purpose is the work of the Holy Spirit, who lives in and through every believer.

We can't be whole and fulfilled unless we're in a right relationship with God, but we also can't experience the vitality God wants for us unless we're overflowing into the lives of others. Giving, serving, and caring for others activates our best motives and efforts. Living outside our self-focused comfort zone is a challenge. It's much easier to be self-absorbed and live only for ourselves. In the quest to help others, it's easy to give up because often others don't appreciate our efforts, or it takes too much time. But there's nothing like seeing God use us to touch a person's life. We all have different gifts, talents, personalities, and experiences, but we all have the same calling: to represent our Savior and King in a lost and broken world. Some are skilled at preaching or leading worship, but everyone can initiate a conversation about God's kindness, offer a cup of cool water to a thirsty soul, give a piece of bread to a famished person, and invest a little time into someone who feels hopeless and abandoned. When we see the power and mercy of God flow from us into another person's life, we complete the circle of grace. In fact, it becomes an unending spiral: we receive, we're filled, we overflow, and then we give. As a result, those who receive from us overflow love into the lives of others. I see this phenomenon every day, and I marvel that God is willing to use me as a channel of His grace. Yes, it's difficult sometimes. Certainly, people can be demanding. But I have to realize God reached out to me when I was difficult and demanding too. He didn't turn His back on me, so I will never turn my back on those around me—even those who are annoying!

HOW TO KNOW

Many of us are so deeply wrapped up in the world's value system that we don't even notice God's upside-down kingdom. The world's way is the only way we know to live. King Solomon recognized this blindness. He warned, "There is a way that seems right to a man, but in the end it leads to death" (Prov. 14:12 NIV 1984). In school, teachers use tests to prompt students to study, not to punish them. In the same way, God tests us to show us how we can grow, not to blast us for how far we still need to go. Here are some tests that reveal the condition of our hearts.

- The pronoun test

  Some people can't stop talking about themselves. Every sentence is peppered with "I," "me," and "mine." When we depend on our own strength and live for our own glory, we are the center of our universe. Carla is good at checking my pronouns. When we got married, I was in the habit of talking about my goals, my plans, and my desires. I often used personal pronouns. I remember her correcting me: "There's no *I* in *us*, *we*, and *our*." I got the message. Our pronouns reveal the focus of our hearts.
- Do others matter?

  If someone made a YouTube video of our current decade, what would the viewers notice about us? Would they see us taking care of our own wants and needs all day, or would they see us looking for opportunities to help others? When we genuinely care for others, we listen so well that we ask second and third questions instead of cutting people off or not paying attention, we offer to help with the dishes or other chores, we notice those who are hurting and move toward them instead of seeing them as nuisances, and we gladly serve wherever we can.

Paul told the Philippians, "Do nothing out of selfish ambition or vain conceit, but in humility consider others better than yourselves. Each of you should look not only to your own interests, but also to the interests of others. Your attitude should be the same as that of Christ Jesus" (Phil. 2:3–5 NIV 1984). He didn't say, "Don't *ever* look out for your own interests." He knew we would have to take care of business, but a test of authentic faith is our desire, capacity, and action to go beyond self-interests. The bar is high. If we consider others better than ourselves, it means we meet their needs with the same creativity, the same passion, and the same tenacity with which we meet our own.

Do we love the people God loves? And do we love them the way Christ loves them—joyfully, hopefully, and sacrificially? *Love*, as Jesus defined it and exemplified it, is the willingness to lay down our lives for our friends, and Jesus didn't have a narrow definition of friends. He considered all sinners to be His friends.

- Responding to difficulties

  If we're self-focused, we whine and complain about anything that blocks our immediate gratification. When we have short fuses, we don't have any patience for problems—especially problem *people*! But a person who has God's perspective and values realizes every setback is an opportunity to grow, to experience God's love and power more deeply, and to show others that God can be trusted even in the hardest of times. An upside-down life is revealed when we trust God more than ever—even when others abandon us or blame us.

- Responding to offenses

God wants us to forgive those who hurt us. We can only do that to the extent that we experience God's unlimited forgiveness for our sins. Then His forgiveness overflows from us to those who have let us down. Instead of harboring bitterness, we pray for those who persecute us and show patience to those who get in our way.

This isn't just a bland theological statement; it's an upside-down way of life. Sometimes we feel unjust things happen in our lives undeservedly. Maybe a person at work thwarted you from getting a promotion—one you were expecting to get and worked hard to earn. You counted on the raise and looked forward to the acclaim. Suddenly, all that hard work feels meaningless. But you do have choices. You could attempt revenge on the person who stole the promotion from you. You could mentally relive the painful event over and over again, creating various ways of getting even. Or you could act as if it doesn't bother you—though it's eating you alive! Author and pastor Lewis Smedes wrote, "Vengeance is having a videotape planted in your soul that cannot be turned off. It plays the painful scene over and over again inside your mind . . . And each time it plays you feel the clap of pain again. . . . Forgiving turns off the videotape of pained memory. Forgiving sets you free."[3]

Instead of doing the natural thing—seeking revenge—we can choose to forgive, absorb the pain, and live in freedom from the worry, the bitterness, and the video constantly playing in our minds. We can find the courage and strength to bless the one who hurt us instead of gossiping about him. We can pray for him and ask God to shower His mercy on him. That's a radically different response from what we see in the world. Unfortunately, it's also a very different response from what we see in relationships among believers. God assures us that He can turn tragedy into triumph. As we learn to forgive, we can trust that God has an even better plan for us where we will experience a new sense of hope and joy as we contemplate our future. That is the pinnacle of taking the lid off. That's an upside-down response to heartache.

- Casual conversation and unhurried moments

  What do we talk most effortlessly about with our family and friends, and what is the subject of our thoughts when our minds aren't occupied with other things? The down time in our conversations and thoughts reveals the content of our hearts. Some of us can't wait to tell our friends about our latest purchase, our promotion, the way we were snubbed, or the injustice we recently suffered. And in our quiet moments, our thoughts drift to daydreams of having more acclaim and the latest gadget—or to nightmares of worry, doubt, and resentment.

I'm not suggesting that we should sing praises to God all day every day, but I am suggesting that a sense of wonder at God's majesty and goodness won't be far from our minds or our mouths if our hearts are overflowing with His grace and greatness.

UTTERLY RELEVANT

Recently, I was at a restaurant, having dinner with my daughter, and we had the pleasure of meeting two ladies who were enjoying a girls' night out. After exchanging pleasantries and engaging in small talk, I got around to asking my most popular question: "What church do you attend?" One of them answered that she was a devout and *practicing* Christian who regularly attends church. The other girl apprehensively admitted she wasn't a regular church attendee and rarely spent time in prayer or studying the Bible. However, she was eager to make sure I understood she was a Christian. Some people only dabble with the Christian faith but don't dive in because they don't think Jesus is relevant to their daily lives. They think Jesus is a good teacher and a good example to follow, but not a revolutionary Savior who has the right to turn their lives upside down. And as long as they leave Him on the sidelines, they can't experience all of His power to take the lid off and enjoy their full potential.

Jesus is relevant—utterly and supremely relevant. Every principle, philosophy, and strategy that invites God's favor in a person's life comes through Him. And nothing that has eternal value comes through any other source. The world promises peace and success, but it's just a passing shadow of all God has for us. The path to true favor, however, isn't just a ramped-up version of the world's pattern. It's different—completely and radically different.

Jesus cared more for us than for His own life. Everywhere He went He served. No matter how many times He was ridiculed, misunderstood, or rejected, He kept reaching out to extend the hand of God to every person—the rich and the poor, the up-and-comers and the down-and-outers, the prostitutes and the religious elite, fellow Jews and hated Samaritans, family members and Roman soldiers. To Jesus, no one was off-limits for His outward focus.

When we take steps to align our lives with God's upside-down values, some people will be delighted, some will be confused, and a few will think we've lost our minds. We don't need to get upset when people question us. They wondered about Jesus, and they'll wonder about us. A few years ago, I wrote a song about our conversation with those who doubt Him and us. It's called "So Easy."

> They say, With all the bad that's in the world today
> They say, If God is love then what's with all the hate?
> I say, You can't control your heart but it still beats—it's
> that easy.
> They say, How can you believe what you can't see?
> They say, If he is here then point him out to me.
> I say, You can't see the wind but you still breathe—it's
> that easy.

Don't let the world's voice drown out God's soft whisper of invitation to join Him in the greatest revolution the world has ever known. You and I have the privilege of drawing deeply from the well of God's great love and letting it flow from us to transform the people we touch each day. Take the lid off and let it flow.

> Our human compassion binds us the one to the other—not in pity or patronizingly, but as human beings who have learnt how to turn our common suffering into hope for the future.
>
> —NELSON MANDELA

CONSIDER THESE QUESTIONS

1. Describe the analogies of slavery and addiction to illustrate how the world's system has impacted us.
2. Which of the upside-down statements (within this chapter, from the passage in Matthew 16, or in the Beatitudes) seems most challenging to you? Explain your answer.
3. Read John 7:37–39. How would you define and describe *spiritual thirst*? What does the overflow of the Spirit look like? To what extent are you experiencing this overflow at this point in your life? Do you want more? Why or why not?
4. Which of the tests from this chapter is most difficult for you? Which one are you passing? What are some changes you want to make?
5. If someone told you that Jesus is irrelevant, how would you answer?

FOUR

GIVE YOURSELF AWAY

May God deliver us from self-righteous judging
and make us, instead, merciful carriers of
Christ's salvation and freedom everywhere we go.

—JIM CYMBALA

I DON'T KNOW HOW IT WORKS IN OTHER CHURCHES, BUT AT OUR CHURCH, everybody in the congregation seems to think they're related to my family. When my sons, Tre' and Ashton, were young (five and seven), they received birthday and Christmas gifts from hundreds of people. Sometimes we rented the local skating rink for birthday parties. Children I'd never seen before showed up and brought presents. It was remarkable. I really appreciated the love poured out on them, but at one point, I realized this was a moment to teach them an important lesson.

Carla and I wanted our boys to enjoy the presents, but we also wanted to be sure their hearts didn't become focused more on the gifts than on the Giver. It's a challenge in all our lives to "keep the main thing the main thing." God tests us often to see where our treasure lies, so we decided to give Tre' and Ashton a little test. After one of these blowout parties, we filled the backs of three SUVs with presents, but we didn't go home. We drove our little caravan to a facility that takes donations for needy children in the Chicago area. When we stopped, I told the boys they could each pick out three presents to keep. They looked at me as if I'd lost my mind. This was the moment I'd been waiting for. I explained that God had richly blessed them, but He always blesses so we can be a blessing to others. We decided to donate all the rest of the gifts to children in need.

At first they looked confused, but within minutes they completely accepted the plan. Tre' and Ashton trusted Carla and me. They knew we loved them and every decision—even those they didn't immediately understand—was for their best. They had confidence we would provide for them. But there was another reason the boys gladly watched their toys being carried into the facility: they'd seen the poverty of numerous families, and they realized they could play a part in relieving suffering and bringing some joy to boys and girls their ages. Suddenly, all the talks, messages, and conversations about caring for the poor ceased to be academic. In that moment, our sons became joyful givers.

Carla and I wondered if this lesson would be just a flash and then forgotten. Before the big birthday party the next year, the boys came to us with their own plan. They'd seen ads for St. Jude's Children's Hospital, and they were curious about it. They asked what was wrong with those boys and girls on the television screen, and we explained that they were very sick. Both agreed to reach out to these kids and stated, "This year, we want all the gifts to go to St. Jude's. Is that all right with you?"

All right? It was magnificent! My heart just about exploded with joy and gratitude. Then I wondered where this idea came from. I looked at Carla with that look that every couple knows. She shrugged and said, "It's not me. I didn't have anything to do with it."

But they weren't done. A few months later, Ashton announced

that he wanted to collect clothing for people in our community who had only worn, dirty, old clothes to wear. A culture of generosity was forming in our family. (If I had died that day, I would have been fulfilled. Nothing has brought me more joy than what my sons did and continue to do for others.)

My parents had modeled this kind of generosity in our family. When I was a boy, I gladly gave anything I had to kids in need. In fact, they may have modeled gracious giving too well. On several occasions, I gave a new shirt or even my lunch money away to kids I had just met, and my mother was not happy. She said, "Son, you can't give *everything* away!"

No, not everything, but a lot of things. That's what I'd learned from her and my dad, even if she was concerned that I was taking it too far. For them, for me, for Carla and our kids, grace-infused generosity isn't just what we do; it's who we are as followers of the ultimate Giver. And as anyone who has had children knows, giving doesn't come naturally. Among the first words babies speak is "Mine!" Giving has to be taught and modeled if it's going to take hold.

GYA: GIVE YOURSELF AWAY

Authentic generosity requires heart transformation. When we realize we are rich beyond measure, we open our hands to give generously to others. As long as we view ourselves as impoverished or having less than those we admire, we cling to our time, talents, and treasure. We may give, but these acts are isolated and begrudging events. They don't come as a natural overflow of love and grace from the depths of our hearts. When our hearts are captured by the unfathomable grace of God, we daydream more about giving than about getting. We seek opportunities to help people in need instead of impressing our friends with new possessions.

One of the most powerful principles of spiritual life is that when we try to acquire things, we lose them, but when we give generously, God pours out His blessings on us. It's not always immediate, and it may not be in kind, but we can be sure that God always rewards grace-directed, heartfelt generosity. I saw this principle lived out every day in my parents' lives, and Carla and I have seen it in our family. When our boys caught on so profoundly, I realized anyone could give this way. I wanted to impart it to every person in our faith community. We call it GYA: give yourself away. It's not just about giving away things that are expendable, the things we don't want or need any longer. It's about giving ourselves wholly and joyfully to God in response to His limitless generosity to us. After that, generosity becomes more spontaneous and natural.

In Paul's second letter to the Corinthians, he wanted to motivate them to help the believers who were suffering from famine in Palestine. He gave them an example. Around the coast of Greece was another church that had made a commitment to give. These people weren't giving out of their surplus. They were digging into near-empty pockets to find some money to donate. Paul described them, their commitment, and their hearts:

> And now, brothers, we want you to know about the grace that God has given the Macedonian churches. Out of the most severe trial, their overflowing joy and their extreme poverty welled up in rich generosity. For I testify that they gave as much as they were able, and even beyond their ability. Entirely on their own, they urgently pleaded with us for the privilege of sharing in this service to the saints. And they did not do as we expected, but

> they gave themselves first to the Lord and then to us in keeping with God's will. (2 Cor. 8:1–5 NIV 1984)

The Macedonian Christians didn't wait until their bank accounts were full before they gave. And they didn't give as a single event and hope that was the end of it. Their incredible generosity came out of a heart filled and overflowing with God's grace. They "gave themselves first to the Lord." They were His, they knew Him, and they wanted to act like Jesus in giving everything they had for God and His kingdom's cause.

People respond to teaching, but even more, they respond to the powerful combination of teaching and modeling. That's how Christ taught: He spoke to thousands, and then He lived out what He had taught as He met people along the way. I had seen my parents give themselves to the Lord and then to other people. Likewise, our boys had watched as Carla and I gave generously. In fact, the rule in our family is that no one can receive anything for Christmas until he has first given to others in need. This wasn't a harsh demand imposed on our boys. It was a principle that emerged from them seeing the fruit of their own generosity. Because they'd seen it, the "rule" was a heart commitment, not a demand they resented.

But of course, the human heart always leans toward selfishness. Before these events, Carla and I gave our boys big empty bags for the toys they were going to give away. After they put stuff into the bags, we inspected them. Sometimes, we found broken toys, torn books, and other useless stuff. I told them, "This isn't generosity. You're just throwing junk away!" I told them to go back and think about the kids who would receive their things. I explained, "You can't give things that are worthless. You need to give things that will bring as much joy as you had when you first played with them.

What reaction would you want to see on their faces, sheer joy or disgust?" This question seemed to make a difference in clarifying their motivation.

One year, the boys tested us. We gave them the bags, but they found excuses to avoid filling them up. Carla and I both explained (again) the meaning of giving and the heart of generosity. We told them we sow into the lives of others so God can sow into ours. They still seemed hesitant, so we gave them a deadline to fill up their bags. The deadline came and went, but the bags remained empty. One day when they were at school, I went into their rooms and put their toys—all of them—into the bags. I carefully hid the bags in the garage where I knew they'd never look. When they came home that afternoon, you would have thought the world had come to an end! Their response showed me that they had forgotten the reason for generous giving. For a couple of months, Carla and I let them moan and cry about the loss of their toys. We listened, and then we shrugged and said, "If you want to receive, you first have to give."

Finally, when the time was right, I got the bags of toys out of the garage and returned the toys to Tre' and Ashton. By this time, I was sure they had learned their lesson, and I was right. From that day, they've given themselves to the Lord, and they've had an open hand with all their possessions.

Tests don't happen only to little boys in the Norful household. God tests all of us to see where our hearts are. Sometimes He allows our most treasured possessions to be taken away, or we don't get something on which our hearts have been set for a long time. These instances aren't God's mistakes; they're classrooms where He wants to teach us His foundational lessons. The answer, though, isn't simplistic. It's not a simple business deal that promises we'll make more than we invest. More than anything else, God wants our hearts. When we experience the wonder of His generosity in grace, hope, and love, things become far less important. We treasure Him, not them. Instead of demanding more and better stuff, we long to use everything we possess to make a difference.

As a parent, I love to give to thankful children. God is no different. He delights in showering blessings, favor, and every form of riches on His sons and daughters who care far more about Him than about the things He gives them.

THE PROMISE

My parents understood it. Carla and I have lived it. Our boys faced the test and passed it. And every believer knows the tension of living in this world but having a heart for another kingdom. We need assurance that taking the lid off our generosity is worth it, and God gives us a magnificent promise. In his letter to the Corinthians, Paul encouraged them:

> Remember this: Whoever sows sparingly will also reap sparingly, and whoever sows generously will also reap generously. Each man should give what he has decided in his heart to give, not reluctantly or under compulsion, for God loves a cheerful giver. And God is able to make all grace abound to you, so that in all things at all times, having all that you need, you will abound in every good work. . . . Now he who supplies seed to the sower and bread for food will also supply and increase your store of seed and will enlarge the harvest of your righteousness. You will be made rich in every way so that you can be generous on every

> occasion, and through us your generosity will result in thanksgiving to God. (2 Cor. 9:6–8, 10–11 NIV 1984)

Could the promise be any clearer? Many Christians are like the man who wanted to hold sand in his hand. As he squeezed it more tightly, more of it fell out. When we squeeze our possessions, money, and other resources, we miss out on the incredible blessings of God. Holding them with a death grip blocks the flow of the Spirit and impoverishes the harvest of righteousness, joy, and plenty. Sowing gladly, sacrificially, and generously opens the floodgates of God's favor.

The cycle of blessing and generosity need never end. God keeps pouring out His blessings on us, and out of hearts filled with thanks, we channel His blessings to people in need. First, we give ourselves to the Lord; then we sow our possessions into the lives of others. God blesses us even more. That's not my promise; it's God's. You can depend on Him to come through.

Today, many people seem to be satisfied with merely surviving. They've suffered heartaches and setbacks, and their vision is clouded by disappointments. They seem only to want to get by. But God wants more for us than that—much more. He doesn't want us to *survive.* He wants us to *thrive*! He has equipped us with the truth of His Word, the power of the Holy Spirit, and the exalted purpose of representing Him to the world around us. We have the unspeakable privilege of being coheirs with Christ, partners in the greatest enterprise the world has ever known. God's heart, His plans, and His resources are unlimited. At the end of a beautiful prayer in his letter to the Ephesians, Paul ended with a flourish about the sufficiency of God: "Now to him who is able to do immeasurably more than all we ask or imagine, according to his power that is at work within us, to him be glory in the church and in Christ Jesus throughout all generations, for ever and ever! Amen" (Eph. 3:20–21). God is able. No matter what we face, God is more than able to meet our needs in a way that shines the light of attention and admiration on His glory.

We live in an age of instantaneous results. We have astounding technology in our hands that, with only a few keystrokes, can connect us with virtually anyone in the world and access the acquired knowledge of humankind. Spiritual life, though, isn't like that. The Bible often uses agricultural metaphors to describe a life of faith: sowing and reaping, spring rains and droughts, pruning, herding sheep, bearing fruit, and many others. All of these take time and involve a process. We may want God to give us immediate solutions, but He has a purpose in the process. In fact, God often wants to teach the most important lessons of endurance, steadfast faith, and trusting the unseen instead of the seen as we wait for His answers to our initial request.

We often miss God's blessings because we don't endure in our faith. The children of Israel had been miraculously freed from slavery in Egypt. God had sent ten plagues to soften Pharaoh's heart so he would let them go. When they left the gates of Egypt, they took gold and silver and other precious things. The slaves became rich! At the Red Sea, Pharaoh's army threatened to destroy them, but God made a way through the sea for them. Then, the spies brought back word of the Promised Land. The fruit was so big they had to carry grapes on poles suspended between two men! It was all there for the taking, but the people's fear eroded their faith.

We may shake our heads as we read this sad story, but in reality, we're a lot like them. God has given us "precious and magnificent promises," but His path to them often involves confusing delays and disappointments. These obstacles are tests of our faith—in

God, in His path, and in His timing—but many people fail the tests and bail out before the blessings come.

Delays—especially in our instant-access culture—stir up doubts and fears that God isn't going to come through. But delays simply mean that God has multiple agendas that He's weaving together into a beautiful and strong fabric. God is never in a hurry. He took hundreds of years to fulfill the promise of the Messiah in Israel when Jesus was born in Bethlehem. And it's been almost two thousand years since Jesus promised to return, and He's still not back yet.

Peter (who wasn't exactly known for his patience) learned a thing or two as a leader of the church. He wrote two letters to people who had been thrown out of Palestine and suffered as exiles. They wanted relief, and they wanted it now, but Peter reminded them, "Do not forget this one thing, dear friends: With the Lord a day is like a thousand years, and a thousand years are like a day. The Lord is not slow in keeping his promise, as some understand slowness. Instead he is patient with you, not wanting anyone to perish, but everyone to come to repentance" (2 Peter 3:8–9).

In nature, everything happens in due season. Birds fly south in the fall and back north in the spring. Trees, flowers, grapevines, and other plants burst forth in blossoms in the spring, thrive in the summer, and die back or lose leaves in the fall. During the winter, they may look dead, but they're not. They're getting ready for a new season of growth and plenty. There are seasons in our lives too. If we don't recognize that fact, we become deeply discouraged in autumn and winter periods in our families, careers, health, and friendships. The children of Israel died at the edge of their destiny. They didn't understand the process of moving *to* the land, *into* the land, and *over* the land God had promised them. They thought God would magically kill all their enemies. He was going to defeat the enemy, but He was going to use His people to do it. They wanted an easy, instant solution, but God gave them a process.

AMOUNT AND MOTIVE

Sometimes, we become discouraged because we are unable to give more. We may compare ourselves with others in our church who give a lot, and we realize we're not even close. The amount we give matters, but only in light of our motives. Giving out of surplus may impress the people sitting next to us in church, but it doesn't impress God. Paul said that he was amazed at the generosity of the Macedonians because they gave "in rich generosity" "out of the most severe trial" and "extreme poverty." They didn't resent giving to God's work. They gave with "overflowing joy" (2 Cor. 8:2). They may not have been able to give as much as wealthy people, who lived in comfort and prosperity, but God was satisfied with their gift.

Jesus made the same point when He took His followers to the temple during the week before He was arrested and executed. The temple treasury was located in the court of the women. There, the priests placed thirteen trumpet-shaped containers that rang out when people threw coins into them—the more and bigger the coins, the louder they rang. People listened and watched as each person dropped in his or her contributions. Mark puts us on the scene looking over the shoulders of Jesus and His disciples:

> Jesus sat down opposite the place where the offerings were put and watched the crowd putting their money into the temple treasury. Many rich people threw in large amounts. But a poor widow came and put in two very small copper coins, worth only

> a few cents. Calling his disciples to him, Jesus said, "Truly I tell you, this poor widow has put more into the treasury than all the others. They all gave out of their wealth; but she, out of her poverty, put in everything—all she had to live on." (Mark 12:41–44)

I don't know what the disciples had been watching as they sat together that day, but we can be sure that Jesus was watching the people who brought their donations. He noticed that some who brought the most gave only for show. They wanted everyone to hear the loud clang in the container and look over to notice them. Jesus wasn't impressed with their motivation. The amount they gave may have been large to some of us, but it was a tiny fraction of their income. And they gave it with selfish motives. We can almost hear Jesus sigh as He noticed the poor old widow who shuffled up to the container. Her two little coins hardly sounded when she dropped them in. But her quiet generosity demonstrated faith that amazed Jesus. There aren't many things that amazed Him, but this generous lady captured His heart that day.

Does our giving capture His heart? Does our quiet generosity amaze Him? Or are we more like the rich religious people who gave to be noticed by their friends instead of to win the applause of heaven? The amount we have in our bank accounts doesn't matter. Nothing can prevent us from being joyful, generous givers—nothing but selfishness, ignorance, fear, and doubt.

RISKS AND JOYS

Even when we give, we have to realize that our hearts can mislead us. Like the rich religious leaders in the temple that day, we can give to impress people instead of to please God. I have attended churches where the offering was published so everyone knew who gave what, and the number on that piece of paper determined each person's prestige, honor, and power. The ones who gave a lot expected their votes and voices to carry extra weight in any decision. This false piety produced fierce pride. These people expected pastors to jump when they spoke.

When I became a pastor, I decided that giving should have no strings attached. This frustrated some people, since it took away their perceived power, but the decision liberated the church and me to follow God without being held hostage by a few rich people in the congregation. When a few of them tried to use their giving to get me to side with them on an important decision, I said gently but clearly, "Thank you for what you give. I'm sure you're giving it to God, and He's pleased. I appreciate your perspective about this decision. I'll certainly consider your point of view." But I never factored their giving into the decision-making process. Sooner or later, they realized this. Some were angry, but others were relieved that I was going to live under God's hand and not man's thumb.

We can also give in a foolish attempt to get leverage with God. If we give, we may wrongly assume, God owes us. That kind of thinking reveals a religious but selfish spirit, not a grateful heart overflowing with generosity. Sometimes, wrong motives lead to terrible outcomes. That was the attitude of the Pharisees in Jesus' day. He tried hard to correct their thinking, but eventually, they plotted to kill Him.

Another error we can make in our giving is to give to the wrong causes. Not every person who asks for help deserves our resources. We need wisdom and persistence to examine each opportunity and discern if the organization is trustworthy and if God's call in our lives matches the organization's calling. Giving money to unworthy causes is like giving money to an addict. We may feel good about the gift, but it ruins the recipient. And sometimes it ruins us. I've made this mistake. At one point I was so committed to giving that I invested my heart, my time, and my resources in every cause that showed up in my office (and a few that I went looking for). I thought I was doing exactly what the Lord wanted me to do, but I wasn't being wise. I became so emotionally and physically exhausted that I lost my voice for almost seven months. I was giving to everybody, but I became no good to anybody. I was so confused. How could this happen when I was giving God my all? Finally, it dawned on me that God wanted me to add wisdom to my generosity. I needed to be more selective in sowing seeds into other people and other organizations. It was a lesson I'll never forget.

When we give foolishly, we're sowing our seed in poor soil, which delays or denies the harvest we might have expected. It's not enough just to give. We need to become shrewd stewards of the resources God has entrusted to us.

As we've seen, impatience in our giving inevitably leads to disappointment—with God and maybe with the people who represent God. Many people have been taught that God blesses their giving, but they may have missed the principle that seasons and delays are often part of the process.

Into our instant culture and selfish hearts, God promises the richest of blessings. Jesus, our King and Savior, is the first and greatest blessing. He gave Himself to us—completely, unconditionally, with no strings attached. He gave up His glory, His peace, His comfort, and His life to pay the ultimate sacrifice for us to be adopted into God's family. Jesus had no conditions on His generosity to us. When we begin to grasp the depths of His love and grace, we can become a little more like Him.

Some of us give with strings attached: we'll give, but only if God will give us what we want when we want it. Grace changes everything. As we experience the fullness of Christ's love for us, we offer love and service with no games, no manipulation, no power grabs, and no impatience when results are delayed. We can trust that God will always fulfill His promises—maybe not in our time frame, but certainly in His.

Some of the greatest thrills of my life happen when I know God has used me to bless another person's life. I've seen people's eyes light up when they understand that a truth from God's Word makes a difference to them. I've gotten thousands of notes from people who tell me my songs have inspired them. I've watched leaders find their places and excel, and I've seen broken people experience God's healing power. Every time I sense God using me as I give a little, I'm refreshed, charged up, and excited to give even more. Who else can I reach? Who else can I touch? God, let your blessings flow into all of us and through us!

When I give myself away and see God use me, I have the distinct joy of knowing my life matters. By God's grace, I've made a difference. This feeling reminds me that I'm accomplishing something that will last forever. Each changed life is a trophy of God's mercy. The day we saw more than one hundred people stand at the altar and give their lives to Christ is more valuable than all the statues and awards I'll ever receive.

My friend and mentor Dr. Sam Chand came to our house one day. Carla and I showed him around. After a while, he asked, "So, Pastor Smokie, where are your trophies?"

I pointed to a room we had just left and said, "A couple of them are in that room. Some others are on a shelf in this room."

He asked, "What about the Grammys?"

I reached behind some other statues, picked up a Grammy, and blew the dust off it. I was a little embarrassed that it wasn't sparkling clean and shining for him. I just held it out and said, "Here it is."

The other statues on the shelf in front of it were my sons' trophies for karate, T-ball, and soccer. Their accomplishments were—and are—every bit as important as mine—even more.

Dr. Chand looked at it for a second. Then he looked at my sons' trophies and said, "Wow!"

I don't think he was amazed at the Grammy. He was surprised that I valued my sons' accomplishments more than my own. But that's what grace does to a person's heart. (And this was definitely the result of grace. Apart from grace, I'd have probably built a showroom for myself.) The love of God fills us so we don't have to jockey for position, we don't have to wear masks to impress people, and we don't feel compelled to put others down to bring ourselves up. We are whole and complete in the love, power, and mercy of God; therefore, we can offer honor, money, time, and every ounce of skill we possess to those who need it. We can take the lid off and give as the Macedonians did: first to God, and then to others—including our families, neighbors, churches, and coworkers. Giving to others displays a powerful message of love. Our humble acts of service and generosity—even a kind word to a discouraged heart—display the character of Christ to those who receive our gifts. I know I'm valuable to Jesus because He gave Himself for me in the ultimate way. People know they're valuable to us when we give them our attention, our affection, and our abilities. We give this kind of love by the specific acts we do and in the environment we create. I hope my sons realize I value their success more than I value mine. I think they get it. If not, they will someday.

It seems that every new generation thinks they've invented the world. Certainly, modern people have come up with new technology and advances in every field of economics, medicine, agriculture, and engineering, but they didn't start from scratch. Whether they realize it or not—and whether they appreciate it or not—they stand on the shoulders of the creative, wise risk-takers and caregivers who came before them. When I see God use me to touch people's lives, I'm amazed that He would let me participate in His redeeming work. Also, I'm very grateful to my parents, their parents, and generations who have shaped who I am. I'm a product of their love, faithfulness, and courage.

Some of us, however, look at our family legacy and cringe. We look back on generations of shame, pain, estrangement, and heartache. In God's wisdom and grace, He turns even the worst legacy into a wonderful lesson. We can build a redeemed legacy on the lessons we learn from life's greatest difficulties. No matter what your heritage may be, God wants to use it for good. Continuing a great tradition begins with gratitude. Changing a painful past into a glorious future begins with insight about God's grace and purposes. No matter where we've come from, God has a bright future for us. Gratitude is the result of experiencing generosity, and it launches new waves of generous giving. Thankfulness and generosity are inextricable.

Do you want your family to walk with God and enjoy warmth, love, and support? Be generous. Do you want people to come to Christ as their Savior? Be generous. Do you want a suffering person to find hope and healing? Be generous. Do you want to fulfill your divine purpose? Be generous. Generosity is the natural expression of a heart filled with God's amazing grace. Be filled, and let it flow.

If you really want to take the lid off, give to those who can't give back. Give to the poor, the struggling families, the weak, the hungry, the thirsty, the homeless, the sick, and the prisoners. Jesus said that those who give to "the least of these" are actually loving and serving Him (Matt. 25:40).

I wish I could bottle the feeling of joy and fulfillment I enjoy when I give myself away. One taste is all it takes to get hooked on it—and it's an addiction that has no downside! If people experience this kind of thrill, they'll never want to go back to a drab, empty life of pursuing wealth, fame, comfort, and power without the Lord.

To give yourself away, you have to have something worth giving to others. First, open your heart and let the love of God fill every part. Be honest about your pain, your sins, and your needs so you can experience the abundance of His grace. Then, out of this wealth of love, take the lid off and give yourself away. The world is waiting for you. The world begins under your roof. Start there.

> Many men go fishing all of their lives without knowing it is not fish they are after.
>
> —HENRY DAVID THOREAU

CONSIDER THESE QUESTIONS

1. Why is it important to first give ourselves to the Lord before we give to others?
2. Do you really believe God delights in our generosity and

pours out His blessings on generous people because He trusts them to use His wealth to change lives? Explain your answer.

3. What is the promise of sowing and reaping in 2 Corinthians 8? Why is it important to realize there are seasons?
4. What are some motives in giving that thrill God's heart? Which motives make Him shake His head? Which of these characterize your current giving?
5. Why do we need wisdom in our generosity?
6. What is your specific response to this chapter? Does it inspire you, confuse you, discourage you, or challenge you?
7. What changes are you going to make—in your heart and in your specific gifts of time, talent, and treasure?

PART 3

UPWARD

FIVE

RELEASE YOUR POTENTIAL

Purpose is when you know and understand what you were born to accomplish. Vision is when you see it in your mind and begin to imagine it.

—MYLES MONROE

MY FRIEND JASON TYSON HAS ALWAYS HAD INCREDIBLE MUSICAL ABILITY. HE WAS my musician and music director even before we planted the church. I could have chosen almost anyone in the country to play for me. I chose Jason. Artists and studios all across the nation recognized his unique talent.

One day, Jason and I sat at my kitchen table to talk about a new album. In the discussion, I realized he isn't only an amazing talent; he's an amazing person. He loves God, he's generous, and he has integrity. Because he's such an authentic, humble person, friends flock to him. His character qualities are just as outstanding as his extraordinary musical abilities.

But Jason was hesitant to take risks. Unlike Peter, he was afraid to step out of the boat and walk on the sea of uncertainty. He was like the other eleven men who hunkered down in the bottom of the boat that night. He preferred to play it safe. He had all the talent in the world, but he didn't have the level of confidence needed to maximize his potential.

Jason had been in church all his life, but no one had painted a picture of the enormously fantastic future for him. No one had invited him to get up, take a risk, and step out of the boat. No one had been standing on those stormy seas, extending a hand to him. No one gave Jason a little shove to help him take the first step toward his full potential in music and ministry. Without the invitation and the push, he most likely would have remained content in the boat. It wasn't that he was a blatant, evil, selfish sinner. He is actually one of the nicest, most incredible believers you will ever meet. However, he was doing everything "ordinary" Christians do. But God doesn't settle for ordinary. He wants us to experience the extraordinary!

Our potential is a product of three overlapping and interconnected factors: character, talent, and faith. If any of these is missing, our potential remains dormant. When all these cylinders are firing, we can go far and fast!

We don't just wake up one day and realize the vast potential God has for each of us. First, we need to look inward to experience God's cleansing. When we are empty and broken, God gladly fills us and heals us in our innermost parts. But God doesn't fill us for our own sake. He wants us to look outward so His love and power can overflow in generous and surprising ways, giving to people in need. When we get a taste of the abundant, powerful, transforming, impacting life God has for us, we can't get enough. We want as much of Him as we can get, and we want Him to use us to the fullest extent. We then look upward. We pray, "Lord, I'm all Yours. Cleanse me. Fill me. Use me. Accomplish Your grand purposes through me!"

The process of maximizing our potential, though, inevitably involves significant tests. The story of Joseph gives us a glimpse of what this might look like.

VISION GIVEN, VISION REALIZED

In the book of Genesis, we learn how God used Joseph to accomplish His will, but the process was not always clear to him, and it often proved emotionally painful. Joseph was Jacob's eleventh son. His mother, Rachel, was Jacob's favorite wife, and Joseph was Jacob's favorite son. (Let me just say that every time polygamy appears in the Bible, it results in strife, division, and chaos. The Bible doesn't endorse polygamy; instead, it depicts clearly the various problems that arise when God's design for the family isn't followed.) Joseph's brothers despised him because he was favored by their father, and they hated him even more when he announced that he'd had two dreams in which his family had bowed down to him. His dreams appeared arrogant, even for our times. Who was he, the eleventh kid, to announce that he would someday rule over his brothers and, even more startling, over his parents (37:1–11)?

One day, Jacob sent Joseph on an errand to check on his brothers, who were tending their sheep in a distant valley. When he showed up, his brothers realized he wasn't under his father's protection. They plotted to kill him, but one of them, Reuben, convinced them to sell him to a passing caravan headed to Egypt. They then lied to their father and told him wild animals had killed Joseph.

When the caravan arrived in Egypt, the merchants sold Joseph to Potiphar, one of Pharaoh's officials and captain of the guard. Joseph was assigned to work closely with Potiphar as head slave in his house. Before long, Potiphar's wife was attracted to the tall, young, handsome Hebrew. She tried to seduce Joseph, but he resisted and fled. She then went to Potiphar and claimed Joseph had tried to rape her. Potiphar must have known better, because the normal punishment for a slave trying to rape his master's wife would have been death. Instead, Potiphar had Joseph thrown into prison (37:12–36; 39:1–20).

Things weren't working out the way Joseph's dreams had predicted!

In prison, Joseph proved to be an asset to the jailer as a talented administrator. While there, he kept trusting God and believed that somehow, someday, God would make things right. He remained a prisoner for more than a decade.

While imprisoned, Joseph was given the role of watching over the other prisoners because he had won the warden's favor. Soon, Joseph's gift of interpreting dreams became known. When the pharaoh's cupbearer and baker were thrown into prison, both of them had dramatic dreams. They asked Joseph to explain the meaning. He told the cupbearer his dream meant he would be restored to his position serving Pharaoh. The baker's dream, however, had a more sinister interpretation. Joseph told him that his dream indicated that Pharaoh would execute him within three days—and it came to pass.

Joseph asked the cupbearer to remember him when he stood at Pharaoh's side, but the servant forgot. As a result, Joseph remained stuck in prison (40:1–23).

Two years later, Pharaoh had two disturbing dreams. He asked his advisers to interpret them, but they couldn't figure them out. Finally, the cupbearer told his master that years before he had known a man in prison with extraordinary abilities to interpret dreams. Pharaoh immediately sent for Joseph.

At that precise moment, Joseph was ready. He had to be cleaned up and put on real clothes, but his heart was completely ready for the assignment God was giving him. He had been betrayed by his brothers, falsely accused by Potiphar's wife, forgotten by the cupbearer, and had languished in prison for decades—but Joseph's heart wasn't hardened by self-pity, resentment, or shame. During all the disappointments and difficulties, he had kept his heart fixed on God's mercy, God's purposes, and the vision God had given him many years before.

Joseph interpreted Pharaoh's dreams. He predicted seven years of bountiful harvest followed by seven years of famine. Pharaoh realized he needed a capable administrator to store the surplus harvest for the years when his nation would be in need. He appointed Joseph, the forgotten prisoner, as the prime minister of Egypt, second in command to Pharaoh (41:1–40).

In the years of plenty, Joseph stored silos of grain. Seven years later, when the famine hit, the people of Egypt were prepared (41:47–57). But a few hundred miles away, the famine threatened Jacob and his family with starvation. The brothers came to Egypt to buy food, but Joseph disguised himself so they wouldn't recognize him. He then tested them to see if their hearts had changed (42:7, 15–20). When he was convinced their hearts had changed, he revealed his true identity to his astonished brothers, and they went back home and brought their elderly father and the whole family to Egypt. They were in the debt of their son and brother. The original vision had finally been fulfilled (43:1–31).

Look back at that moment in the prison when God was secretly working to prepare Joseph for greatness. Each person played an integral part. The warden had recognized Joseph's talents and given him opportunities to use them, even when no one else could see them. The cupbearer also realized Joseph's God-given ability to interpret dreams. From the human perspective, the cupbearer's delay in telling Pharaoh was maddening, but it was all in God's perfect timing. Even the baker played a role. When he was executed, I can imagine everybody who knew that Joseph had accurately interpreted his dream was even more impressed with him. Finally, when the time was right, God launched Joseph to a place of prominence in Egypt. His position and talents saved the nation, and they also saved his own family from starving to death.

Joseph didn't realize his potential when he was a child with an outlandish dream. God took him through many valleys of heartache, discouragement, and loneliness before his potential was fully realized. In the same way, God often takes us through the death of our dream before He resurrects it as something more beautiful and powerful than we ever dreamed possible.

Joseph's heart was ready, but he needed someone to recognize his talents and open the door of opportunity. The jailer, cupbearer, baker, and Pharaoh played that role in his life. Who's playing it in yours? When you're betrayed, abandoned, falsely accused, forgotten, and alone, don't give up. God is preparing you for something special!

INVITATION AND PUSH

Jason Tyson needed someone to recognize his talents and give him the opportunity to use them. God used me to play that role in his life. It was easy for me and everyone else to notice his extraordinary musical abilities. Jason can make a little keyboard sound like a twelve-foot grand piano! Though his musical talents exceeded most people's abilities, I wanted to challenge Jason to take the lid off and see what could happen in his life. One day, I asked him if he'd ever written a song. He shook his head and answered, "No."

I responded, "What do you mean? You're incredible. Surely you've written before."

"No," he repeated. "No one has ever asked me to write."

I announced, "Jason, you're going to be a songwriter. Anybody who can spontaneously come up with beautiful melodies like you can certainly become a songwriter."

He looked uncomfortable and mumbled, "Well, I don't know how."

"Of course you do," I shot back. "Just go home and put some melodies down. You don't have to structure them. I'll do that for you. Just record the tracks, and I'll take it from there."

A few days later Jason sent me an MP3 file of his first tracks. They were fantastic! I restructured them, added some transitions, and made them flow. I told him to go back and do it again with the new outline. His next version was even better! Together, we worked on the song, and it turned out wonderfully. At that point, I wrote the lyrics to the song. It was finished, and the result was amazing. It (and several more we wrote) ended up on my Grammy award–winning album. I'm not sure who was more thrilled, Jason or me!

My invitation and gentle push opened all kinds of doors for Jason. He got credit for writing the song, and he got a nice paycheck. I taught him the ins and outs of music publishing so he would understand the intricacies of that world. Jason was at the beginning of a world of opportunities. He later coproduced my third and fourth albums. I advised, "Jason, because of your heart for God and your desire to serve Him, I'm going to help you reach your full potential. I'm going to put my shoulder in your back and push you as far as God will give me the wisdom and strength to push you."

He smiled and nodded. I wasn't quite finished. I explained, "Here's the challenge: If your feet aren't moving while I'm pushing you, you'll fall flat on your face. You have to prepare for what God is *about to do*, not just stand on what He's *already done*. Do you understand that?"

The expression on his face changed a bit. If he thought I was going to carry him, he now understood it was going to be very different. I was committed to help, but he had to be committed to keep taking bold steps forward. It wasn't going to work any other way.

By definition, a person's potential is something higher and bigger than he has previously experienced. He has to condition his mind and heart to prepare for more, expect more, and have faith that God will send more. The new prayer is, "God, give me the grace to handle Your dream for me. My dream is too small, but Yours is far greater. I want Yours instead of mine."

Jason had all the God-given talent in the world, and his character was impeccable. But it wasn't until we began our conversations about his potential that we realized he didn't have faith that God could do extraordinary things in and through him. The writer to the Hebrews said, "Without faith it is impossible to please God, because anyone who comes to him must believe that he exists and that he rewards those who earnestly seek him" (Heb. 11:6). Jason needed to have new eyes to see God's vision for his life, and he needed someone to see the potential of his life and talents. It wasn't about me. I'm just the one God sent at that time and place to notice Jason's abilities, appreciate his heart, and push him to go higher. I told him, "God sent me to you with this message and this mission. My input into your life is part of God's calling in my life. When I'm pushing you, I'm exercising faith in God's presence and purpose for me. From first to last, in your life and mine, it's all about God. My mission is to help you become the person God wants you to be. It's not to do your work for you or make your life comfortable. It's to notice your talents and push you to release your potential to the glory of God."

Jason's faith in God's vision for his life knocked down walls of self-doubt and opened doors of possibility. I told him to get ready because there are always risks involved when God pours out His favor on people who trust Him for great things. The risks may be internal: envy, pride, and comparison. Or they may be external: accusations, unjust criticism, and jealousy. I told him, "You need to condition your heart so you'll be ready. God's blessing is wonderful, but it can be a heavy load to carry. Get stronger now so you won't be crushed under the new responsibilities and threats of success."

God can take us through seasons of testing and delays before success is apparent. It certainly happened in Joseph's life, and it happened with King David and the apostle Paul. David was anointed king, but he spent years running from King Saul and his army before he wore the crown. Paul had been the archenemy of the church, but Jesus met him on the road to Damascus and changed his life. He went away for several years to study and prepare for the mission God had given him of taking the gospel throughout the Roman Empire. At the height of his ministry, he was thrown in prison on multiple occasions, sometimes for years. Even in the darkest dungeon, Paul realized God was accomplishing His mysterious purposes. In the lives of David and Paul, the gifts and the calling of God seemed hidden during those times of preparation, but their talents and God's purposes hadn't evaporated. They were just waiting for God to open a door of opportunity.

Too often for us, the delays are self-imposed. They aren't seasons of preparation; they are times of doubt and fear. Joseph, David, and Paul weren't shrinking from God's calling when they felt put on the shelf. They were itching to get into the game! Don't make excuses for inaction. If God has put you on the shelf, stay there and learn the lessons He wants to teach you. But if you've put yourself there because you're afraid of taking a risk, the burden of passivity is all on you. Get up, take a step, and watch God work!

NEVER ENOUGH

Many people have outstanding abilities, but their talents aren't sitting on a bedrock of integrity or directed by faith in God. When people value their skills above all, they often use them for selfish gain. Their purposes are to acquire more power, earn more money, flash nicer stuff, and enjoy their version of the good life. They may get rich, but they won't have true wealth. They may have exciting lives, but they don't have true peace. Life has a way of revealing the condition of our hearts. Cancer doesn't care how much money a person has. People can't protect themselves from heartache behind the privacy gates of a mansion. No matter how much people acquire, it's never enough—unless they receive those things as good gifts from God. When our hearts are fixed on Him, we care about the things He cares about, and we love the people He loves. Jeremiah wrote:

> This is what the LORD says: "Let not the wise man boast of his wisdom or the strong man boast of his strength or the rich man boast of his riches, but let him who boasts boast about this: that he understands and knows me, that I am the LORD, who exercises kindness, justice and righteousness on earth, for in these I delight," declares the LORD. (Jer. 9:23–24 NIV 1984)

There's nothing wrong with wisdom, strength, and riches, but these can't fill an empty heart. They were never designed to make us whole. We need to put God in the center of our affections and our ambitions. Knowing, loving, and serving Him is paramount, but it's not about going through the motions. We are amazed at the depths of His tenderness, the ferocity of His justice, and the breadth of His mercy toward sinners like us.

Faith is essential to release our potential. It puts us in touch with the awesome power that created the universe, the love that saves, and the mind that rules over all. Faith connects us with the One who brings healing, hope, success, reconciliation, and prosperity. Without faith, we get mixed up. We put the tail where the head should be and the head where the tail belongs. That would be a funny-looking dog, but it's a tragic picture of a human life.

PULLING THE LEVER

All of our potential is like a mighty ocean held back by floodgates of fear and doubt. We need to pull the lever of faith to open those gates and let the torrent of possibilities sweep into and through our lives. Let me offer several suggestions:

Keep a clean heart

Some people think repentance is only for people convicted of a crime. They see repentance as a degrading, shameful act. This is not accurate. Repentance is the way we keep short accounts with God, clearing out anything and everything that clouds our relationship with Him. Properly understood, repentance reminds us of God's grace and restores our joy. Avoid it? No way! It's essential if we're going to live lives of vibrant faith. This perspective about repentance is as old as Genesis and as new as this moment in time. If you feel shameful about your past, remember that you are never beyond the point of no return. King David committed sins of adultery and murder. To cover up his affair with Bathsheba, he ordered a troop of men into battle so Uriah, Bathsheba's husband, would be killed. But Uriah wasn't the only one slain that day. Many other soldiers died to cover up David's sin. When Nathan the prophet confronted the king, David admitted what he had done, and he wrote one of the most beautiful and poignant psalms. He confessed:

> Let me hear joy and gladness; let the bones you have crushed rejoice. Hide your face from my sins and blot out all my iniquity. Create in me a pure heart, O God, and renew a steadfast spirit within me. Do not cast me from your presence or take your Holy Spirit from me. Restore to me the joy of your salvation and grant me a willing spirit, to sustain me. Then I will teach transgressors your ways so that sinners will turn back to you. (Ps. 51:8–13)

We need to get it right. Shame, confusion, distance, and spiritual lethargy happen when we don't repent. When we find the courage to be honest with God about our sins (and He already knows all about them, so it's not news to Him), we find the refreshment of forgiveness, restored hope, and the joy of a cleansed heart.

To reach your potential, repent whenever the Spirit of God taps you on the shoulder and points out sin, doubt, and selfishness in your life. Unblock the channels of God's power and love.

Keep a clear and focused mind

Some people assume the Christian life is all about spontaneous responses, but they're wrong. Certainly, we sometimes experience the Spirit's surprises, but over and over in the Scriptures, God instructs us to think, consider, ponder, reflect, and know. To walk closely with God and realize our full potential, we have to hone our minds to think God's thoughts and treasure what He treasures. The prophet Isaiah recorded a song for God's people. Part of it reads, "You will keep in perfect peace him whose mind is steadfast, because he trusts in you. Trust in the LORD forever, for the LORD, the LORD, is the Rock eternal" (Isa. 26:3–4 NIV 1984).

We don't have to wonder what God is thinking. He put it down for us in the Bible. When we read it, we're reading God's thoughts expressed from His heart to ours. But it doesn't take much to get our minds off God. We can be absorbed in praise or asking God to show His power in the life of someone we love, but then a mosquito buzzes near our ears, and we get distracted until we can track it down and kill it. Or the phone rings, the wind blows, someone turns on the television, we hear a neighbor's voice, a child whines, or a spouse walks in the door. Many of these distractions are unavoidable, but they can quickly turn our minds from God to something else. We need to learn the discipline of focus.

God uses His Word to renew our minds. It doesn't happen by magic. We read, we study, we talk to friends about what we're learning, we think more about it, and we listen to the pastor preach. Through all of these connections, the Spirit of God uses the Word of God to transform the minds of people of God.

Our thoughts determine our beliefs, our beliefs shape our attitudes, and our attitudes dictate our behavior. We can't neglect our thoughts and still reach our full potential. We can't keep every selfish, lustful, evil thought out of our minds, but we can recognize them and replace them as soon as possible. We have the responsibility to filter everything going into our minds all day every day. Let that filter be the Word of God.

Sharpen your gifts

A dull ax doesn't cut much wood. Similarly, we need to continually sharpen our talents. If you are a gifted administrator, attend seminars to improve your skills. If you're a leader, ask an outstanding leader to mentor you. If you love to preach or sing, take lessons, listen to the best, and strive to improve. If you have gifts of compassion, hone your skills in listening, counseling, and caring for those you love.

Many people have told the story of two men in the forest. Both men had axes and were assigned the job of cutting timber. Early in the morning, they began. After an hour or two, the first man realized his ax was getting dull, so he stopped to sharpen it. The other man laughed at him and said, "You're wasting valuable time. I'm cutting more than you now." Soon, the first man was back at work. With his sharpened saw, he cut down more wood than the other man did. The day continued with one man stopping every hour or so to sharpen his ax while the other man kept using an increasingly dull instrument. By the end of the day, the man who had stopped to sharpen his ax had cut down twice as many trees.

Don't ever stop sharpening your ax. If you're just identifying your talents and gifts, invest some resources in getting off to a great start. Attend online seminars, find a mentor in your business or church, and learn all you can. If you're already sure about the talents God has given you, don't rest on your experience. Strive for more. Be all you can be.

Walk in the Spirit

When we become Christians, the Spirit of God invades and takes up residence in us. It's an amazing thing: throughout the Old Testament, the temple in Jerusalem was the place where heaven and earth met. When Jesus came, He overturned the money changers' tables to announce that He was bringing a new order to the universe. He, not a building, was the place where heaven and earth met. It was a revolutionary concept. When Jesus died on the cross, the heavy veil protecting the Holy of Holies—the place where the high priest entered once a year into the presence of God to offer a sacrifice of atonement in blood—was torn from top to bottom. This signified to everyone that the door was open for every believer to experience the presence of heaven. Then, when Paul wrote to the Corinthians, he took it to the next step. He informed them, "Do you not know that your bodies are temples of the Holy Spirit, who is in you, whom you have received from God? You are not your own; you were bought at a price. Therefore honor God with your bodies" (1 Cor. 6:19–20). I'm sure the people reading this for the first time said, "Wow! *I'm* the place where heaven and earth intersect! *I'm* the temple of the Holy Spirit! I'd better be a good one!"

The Holy Spirit isn't an impersonal force. He grieves. He groans in prayer. His power is quenched by our fear and doubts. Jesus called Him "the Advocate," or in other translations "the Comforter" (KJV) or "the Counselor" (AMP). The Spirit of God stands before the Father and pleads our case, just as Christ pleads for us too (John 14:15–18; 16:5–11; 1 John 2:1–2).

While we're on this earth, we experience the tension between our sinful natures and the Spirit's purpose and power. In his letter to the Galatians, Paul explained, "So I say, live by the Spirit, and you will not gratify the desires of the sinful nature. For the sinful nature desires what is contrary to the Spirit, and the Spirit what is contrary to the sinful nature. They are in conflict with each other, so that you do not do what you want. . . . Those who belong to Christ Jesus have crucified the sinful nature with its passions and desires. Since we live by the Spirit, let us keep in step with the Spirit" (Gal. 5:16–17, 24–25 NIV 1984). Don't be surprised when you experience this conflict. It's part of the Christian life. But don't give in to temptation! Walk in the Spirit, fight hard, and determine to honor God in everything you do. That's how we glorify Him.

Wait on the Lord

God often injects delays into our plans to test us and teach us important lessons. The most important lesson is that He's God, and we're not. He's in control, and we're not. He deserves glory, and we don't. During times of waiting, we often get discouraged and feel confused. In one of the most famous passages in the Bible, the prophet Isaiah first rebukes our doubts and then offers a gracious promise:

> Do you not know? Have you not heard? The LORD is the everlasting God, the Creator of the ends of the earth. He will not grow tired or weary, and his understanding no one can fathom. He gives strength to the weary and increases the power of the weak. Even youths grow tired and weary, and young men stumble and fall; but those who hope in the LORD will renew their strength. They will soar on wings like eagles; they will run and not grow weary, they will walk and not be faint. (Isa. 40:28–31)

Older versions of the Bible, such as the King James Version say, "They that wait upon the LORD shall renew their strength." Some of us think waiting on the Lord makes us passive. It doesn't at all. When a waiter is serving people in a restaurant, he is attentive and active. He notices everything that's going on with his customers, and he actively meets their needs. We're like waiters, but some of us are standing in the corner and refusing to serve. That's not the model of biblical waiting. To wait on the Lord is to expect Him to be great and good, to do magnificent things, and to bless us with all forms of favor. We're on the edge of our seats, watching and longing for God to reveal Himself, and during that time, we're actively involved in serving, praying, giving, and helping others who need the touch of God.

To release your potential, don't interpret delays as God's absence. God is preparing you, other people, or the situation so He can unleash the power of heaven. While you watch and wait, be diligent and hopeful in serving others. God delights in seeing His children trust Him like this, and He loves to pour out His blessings on those who trust Him.

Watch for God's irony

Gideon was probably the most reluctant hero in the Bible. He tried to get out of following God in every way. During the period of the judges, neighboring nations continually harassed God's people. This time, it was the Amalekites and the Midianites. When God told Gideon to free His people, the terrified man set up two tests to see if God would reveal Himself beyond all doubt. Gideon put out a fleece at night. He asked God to have it wet when the ground was dry, then dry when the ground was wet.

God responded and convinced Gideon. He was now sure it was God who had given him the command to fight, so he gathered an army of twenty-two thousand men. God told him that was too many soldiers. If Gideon won the battle, he and his army would think it was their strength that had won, instead of God's power. Gideon sent more than half of them home, leaving ten thousand in his reduced forces.

To God, that was still too many. He told Gideon to take the men down to the river for a drink. Those who knelt down to drink from the water were to go home, and those who brought water in their hands to their mouths and lapped "like dogs" were to remain. When I studied this passage to preach on it, I assumed that God would select those who knelt. After all, throughout the Bible, kneeling is a sign of humility and faith. But those weren't the ones God chose. Ironically, God picked the other guys. As Gideon watched, only three hundred men drank from their hands! He was going to war with a handful of soldiers who acted like dogs! In our day, calling somebody a dog may not be too offensive. We wash, groom, and pamper our dogs, and we spend billions to care for them. But in Gideon's day, dogs were despised. Calling someone a dog was the worst kind of slander. Gideon not only had a very small army—it was an army of despised mongrels!

I can imagine Gideon telling God, "Look, You want me to maximize my potential, don't You? Well, You're taking away most of my resources to accomplish what You want me to do. This makes no sense at all."

I can almost see God smiling. He might have said, "As long as you trust in yourself or in your own resources, you won't trust in Me. I'm stripping you of almost everything so you can't depend on anything but Me. Do you understand?"

The irony wasn't lost on Gideon. He and his little band of men surrounded the enemy at night, blew their horns, yelled and broke pots containing torches. In the confusion, the enemy soldiers started killing one another! Gideon and his three hundred warriors had won one of the greatest military victories in history (Judg. 6–8).

Sometimes we try very hard to gather resources and hone our skills, but God has another plan. He wants our hearts far more than He does our efforts. On some occasions, He will strip us of everything so we depend on Him alone.

Are you reluctant like Gideon? God wants to make you a leader. Are you trusting in your resources and talents? God may want to take away everything so you have to depend on Him. Are the only people around you outcasts and mongrels? That's fine. God will turn them into His warriors to fight for His cause. This is the ultimate upside-down kingdom. To human eyes, it makes no sense, but to God, it's ironic perfection.

We can only release our potential by releasing God's potential. That takes faith. Our faith doesn't have to be perfect, but it has to be honest. Even the faltering, hesitant, confused, and incomplete faith of Gideon was enough. When we admit our weakness, God is ready to come in with power. When Paul was sick and weak, he had to depend on God more than ever. He explained his revolutionized perspective: "But he said to me, 'My grace is sufficient for you, for my power is made perfect in weakness.' Therefore I will boast all the more gladly about my weaknesses, so that Christ's power may rest on me. That is why, for Christ's sake, I delight in weaknesses, in insults, in hardships, in persecutions, in difficulties. For when I am weak, then I am strong" (2 Cor. 12:9–10). When we're stretched to the limits, we turn to God and realize He is more than enough.

ALIGNMENT

When our hearts, talents, and character are in alignment with God's purposes, amazing things happen. We walk with the beautiful blend of humility and confidence. We get to see God's power in action, and we're amazed.

To get into alignment, take the steps we've identified: Make repentance a regular part of your routine so your heart stays clean and receptive. Fill your mind with thoughts about God. Be a sponge to soak in the truth of God's Word, and then let it marinate in your mind and heart all day. Don't just sit idly with your gifts. Identify them, invest in them, and find a mentor to help you fine-tune them. Realize you are a walking, talking temple of God. The Holy Spirit lives in you, and He produces spiritual fruit as you trust Him. The paths of God wind through the valleys and to the mountaintops. As we follow Him, we'll experience unexpected surges of success and discouraging delays when we don't see His hand at work. Have confidence that He's preparing you for greater things. Even in times of waiting, stay active. Through it all, realize that your maximum potential is released only when you are vitally connected with God so that His limitless potential seeps into every pore, trickles into every moment, and explodes into your deepest needs.

This kind of alignment is like playing a piano. We learn it by careful study and practice, but if we don't keep up the practice, our talent fades. We should enjoy God's peace, but we should never relax. Our hearts need to stay steadfast—always searching, longing, looking, waiting, and expecting God to do magnificent things.

> What we do for ourselves dies with us. What we do for others and the world is and remains immortal.
>
> —ALBERT PINE

CONSIDER THESE QUESTIONS

1. Describe the pattern of potential in your own words.
2. "Our potential is a product of three overlapping and interconnected factors: character, talent, and faith." What happens when each one of these is missing from your life?
3. Who has invited you to release your potential? Who has given you a gentle push? How did you respond?

4. Is the concept of repentance attractive to you? Why or why not? Did the description of it in this chapter make it more attractive? Explain your answer.
5. In your daily walk with God, what is the Holy Spirit's part, and what is your part? At this point in your life, how well are you depending on the Spirit, and how well are you doing your part?
6. What was the irony in Gideon's experience? Can you identify times when God stripped you of resources so you'd trust Him more? What happened?
7. Describe the way the factors must be aligned so your potential can be released.

SIX

TRUST GOD, TRY GOD

If Christ lives in us, controlling our personalities, we will leave glorious marks on the lives we touch. Not because of our lovely characters, but because of his.

—EUGENIA PRICE

ONE SUNDAY I PREACHED A SERMON FROM MATTHEW'S GOSPEL, TITLED "According to Your Faith." Jesus had been raising the dead and healing the sick—all in a day's work for the King and Savior! At one point, two blind men joined the crowd following Him. In itself, that's an interesting concept. They couldn't see what was going on, but their heightened sense of hearing picked up every vibe in the crowd. They'd heard the stories of the miracles this man had performed, and undoubtedly they had talked between themselves about the possibility that He might come to their city. I can imagine them saying, "If He comes here, He can restore our sight!"

They stumbled along with the crowd, but they weren't content to just be part of the background noise. They yelled, "Have mercy on us, Son of David!"

Other people might have been following Jesus just to see the show, but these two men trusted Him for more than entertainment. They were physically blind, but their spiritual sight was clear and sharp. When they shouted, they didn't ask for the miracle of sight. They asked for God's mercy. Instinctively, they knew that the mercy of God opened the door to all other possibilities.

By this time, the number of people around Jesus must have been in the hundreds, probably thousands. In Matthew's account, Jesus didn't stop and go back to meet the blind men. He may not have heard their cries. He went into a house, which is a family's sanctuary of peace and safety. The two blind men didn't care. They wouldn't stop until they had met Jesus! They must have found someone to help them weave their way through the milling crowd to find the door to the house. They barged in unannounced but warmly welcomed.

If I'd been one of those men, I would have had plenty of questions: "Why did You let this happen to me in the first place?" "Didn't You hear us on the road? We yelled to You, but You didn't stop. What's that about?" "What are You doing in this house? We had a hard time finding You. Maybe You didn't realize it, but we're blind!" But they didn't ask any of those questions, and they didn't complain about their condition. They simply and quietly approached the presence of God.

If they had asked why He didn't stop when they called out to Him, He might have told them, "You wanted Me to go where you were, but I wanted you to come where I am. That's the essence of what it means to follow Me."

Jesus didn't have to ask them what they wanted. It was plainly apparent. He simply asked about their faith: "Do you believe that I am able to do this?"

I can imagine their hearts almost bursting with anticipation. They instantly answered, "Yes, Lord."

Do you see the faith in their answer? They didn't just say, "Yes."

They said, "Yes, *Lord*." They realized Jesus wasn't a carnival sideshow doing tricks. He was the promised Messiah, the Son of David, Jehovah, the King of Glory in the flesh! Nothing is impossible for Him!

Jesus probably smiled as He reached over to touch their clouded, blind eyes and said, "According to your faith let it be done to you."

Immediately, the two men could see!

At this early part of Jesus' career, He was afraid that His popularity might cause people to try to make Him king too early. To protect the little anonymity He had left, He told the men, "See that no one knows about this."

Fat chance. That ain't happening. As soon as the two men walked out the door, they told everybody in the region what Jesus had done for them! (Matt. 9:27–31). These two men didn't let anything—including their condition, their established lifestyle of begging, the size of the crowd, or the seeming indifference of Jesus when they yelled to Him—stop them from pursuing God's best for their lives. They were tenacious.

When I spoke on this passage, I explained that we might have dozens of excuses to stand on the side of the street while God's miraculous power and love pass by. We may call out and hope God will answer. When He doesn't, we feel even more like victims of our circumstances. The two men in this passage refused to remain victims any longer. Even when their shouts for help weren't immediately answered, they kept trusting, kept hoping, and kept following until they were in the presence of Jesus and He met their deepest needs—first, mercy; second, sight.

When people see themselves as victims, they find plenty of excuses. But I've seen those with severe physical handicaps, single moms, unemployed workers, the elderly, the sick, and those with all kinds of other very real problems find the courage to be like these two men. They refused to look inside for excuses, and they refused to listen to those who told them it was too late for God to do anything significant in their lives. They kept reaching for Jesus no matter what. Their trust couldn't be quenched by doubts—their own or others'.

I trust that after reading this far God has put a dream in your heart or rekindled one that was once dormant. Now it's time to act. The dream may need to be shaped, pruned, and refined, but it will capture your heart and give you a reason to get up each morning. You won't realize the dream if you simply stand on the sidelines, listening to all the doubters. You have to *trust God.* Then, take action to *try God.* He will respond to your faith. So, get out there and demonstrate your faith by taking a courageous step toward your dreams.

When I preached the message titled "According to Your Faith," there was a man named Malcolm whose heart was deeply touched. I saw Malcolm in the sanctuary that morning. He was looking very intently at me as I spoke. I didn't know what was going on in his mind and heart, but I soon found out. He didn't wait to call me on Monday. The phone rang that same Sunday afternoon. He was so excited! Malcolm had wanted to take the lid off and reach his full potential, but he had been afraid to take the first step. As he listened that day, he realized that if two blind men could have faith for Jesus to restore their sight, he could find the faith to take a step too. He explained, "Pastor, since I was a young man, I've wanted to start my own transportation business. Every time I came close, fears flooded my mind and paralyzed me." He had worked for a transportation company and had contributed to its success. He knew he could run his own business, but until that morning's message, he couldn't find the faith to pull the trigger.

He explained that he had wanted to talk to me a number of

times about his idea, but he was afraid I might think he was foolish. He was shocked when I told him, "Do it! If you're convinced God is telling you to start your own business, by all means, do it." I asked him some questions to be sure he had counted the cost and had a sound business plan. He did, and my affirmation gave him additional confidence.

As Malcolm launched his new venture, we talked several times about managing different elements of the business. I told him, "Get ready for the stresses you'll experience when your business takes off. There are always unexpected joys and trials. Be ready for them. Don't be naive. Be alert and shrewd. Prepare your heart and acquire skills now for the challenges you'll face tomorrow. To do all God has assigned you to do, you'll need the disciplines of prayer, Bible study, and reflection. You will also need to prepare to face challenges and tests. They're coming. You can count on it."

Malcolm responded to God's prompting with a wonderful blend of dynamic faith, hard work, and real wisdom. His dream quickly took shape, but the trials appeared just as I'd warned him. One year later, he told me, "Pastor, I'm really glad you told me what to expect. This has been the hardest season of my life."

When a business looks at résumés and interviews applicants for a job, the HR department looks at each person's qualifications. The HR director wants to know if the applicant's experience and training fit the role in the company. Our trials and difficulties—or, more accurately, our response to those trials and difficulties—show if we are qualified for a higher role in God's kingdom. God isn't going to put unqualified people in key roles. It is our job to realize that every setback, every discouragement, and every criticism is a test. We may think we're testing God to see if He's faithful, but in reality, He's testing us to see if we are the faithful ones.

HOLY DISCONTENT

Jesus is anything but simplistic. He is the Lamb of God as well as the Lion of Judah. He is exquisitely tender and terrifyingly fierce. Jesus came to give us His peace, but a sure mark of spiritual vitality is a nagging, gnawing sense of "holy discontent." A few years ago, Bill Hybels, pastor of Willow Creek Community Church in Chicago, taught that every leader and, in fact, every believer, should be gripped with the fact that the way things are isn't the way they should be. God originally created a perfect world of love, prosperity, and joy, but sin has tarnished His good intentions. Jesus came to redeem the world and make things right. But until He comes again, things aren't complete. Today, we hold God's magnificent promises in one hand and unmet needs in the other. If the crushing hurts of others don't bother us, we aren't in touch with the One who trembled with compassion when He met those who were crippled, poor, sick, and blind. Hybels quoted the cartoon character Popeye. When his frustration finally reached its limit, he blurted out, "That's all I can stands, I can't stands no more!" It may sound strange, but we need to be like Popeye—outraged at injustice, yet gentle, wise, and loving in our response to it. Holy discontent finds expression in bold action to meet the desperate needs of others.

Jesus displayed holy discontent and righteous indignation when He confronted the Pharisees, refused to be bullied by the crowds, healed on the Sabbath, and turned over the tables of the money changers in the temple. In each of these instances (and many others), His outrage was never out of control. It was measured, articulate, and focused on the specific problem.

Often, our sense of discontent is self-focused. We aren't getting something we think we deserve, and it bothers us so much we can't sleep, can't eat, and can't get it out of our minds. Holy discontent is other-centered. We may not be able to sleep or eat, and we may not be able to get it out of our minds, but our thoughts are consumed with finding a way to help people in need. Holy discontent draws out our creativity and passions. Most of the time, the issue we're upset about aligns with the talents and gifts God has given us. He has picked us for *the burden* because He has given us *the ability* to meet the need. Needs come in all shapes and sizes: A person is in trouble. A system isn't working. A group of people is being neglected. A social issue needs to be addressed. Some needs are inside the church; many are outside in the community. People are going hungry, homeless, and without medical care. Some are in our neighborhoods, and some are on the other side of the world. Whatever the case, we can't stand it because the people God loves have needs that aren't being met. God rarely (if ever) puts a need on our hearts that He doesn't use us to meet. If your heart is broken by the plight of others, you can be sure God wants you to take steps to help them. You may not become the key player in the plan, but God will use you in an extraordinary way. God has already invested the answer to the problem by giving you the heart, experience, and skills to meet the need. You just have to trust God and watch Him be faithful to use you.

When David was a young shepherd and heard the taunts of the Philistine giant, Goliath, he asked, "What will be done for the man who kills this Philistine and removes this disgrace from Israel? Who is this uncircumcised Philistine that he should defy the armies of the living God?" (1 Sam. 17:26).

David's brave questions didn't earn respect from those who heard him. But he didn't care. And when King Saul heard that a boy was willing to risk his life to fight Goliath, he sent for him. Saul gave David his own armor, but it was too big and cumbersome.

More important, David wasn't going to fight according to another man's resources. He was going into battle with the tools, skills, and passion God had put in his heart. He was saying, "I can't trust what God has given you. Let me trust what He has put into my heart and my hands. That's *all* I need, and it's *exactly* what I need." David took his sling out of his pocket and picked up five smooth stones. Then he marched out into the valley. As David walked toward the giant, he called out defiantly:

> You come against me with sword and spear and javelin, but I come against you in the name of the LORD Almighty, the God of the armies of Israel, whom you have defied. This day the LORD will deliver you into my hands, and I'll strike you down and cut off your head. Today I will give the carcasses of the Philistine army to the birds of the air and the beasts of the earth, and the whole world will know that there is a God in Israel. All those gathered here will know that it is not by sword or spear that the LORD saves; for the battle is the LORD's, and he will give all of you into our hands. (1 Sam. 17:45–47)

Holy discontent, indeed! David didn't look at his *relative* size. He looked at God's *immeasurable* size and power. With that faith, he found the courage to do the impossible. He placed a rock into his sling and hurled it. The stone struck Goliath in the forehead, and he fell to the earth with a giant *thud*. David cut off his head and held it up as a trophy to God's faithfulness.

We may not have literal, beastly giants walking across a valley to kill us, but we have many kinds of Goliaths in our world too. Like David, when we realize what's happening, we're outraged: *What do you mean there are thousands of people living in the gutters and culverts of every major city in our country? What do you mean that a large percentage of our nation's children are living in poverty and don't have enough clothes or food? What do you mean that half of all marriages end in divorce, devastating the children as much as the couples? What do you mean that many of our schools are underperforming and some kids graduate but still can't read? What do you mean that people in Africa and South America are dying of diseases that require medicines costing only a few cents, but these are unavailable? What do you mean that parts of our cities are unsafe because drug-funded gangs rule the streets? What do you mean that people walk through the doors of our churches each week with crushing needs but don't tell anybody and don't receive the help they need? What do you mean that countless people lack basic training to get them a better job?*

These, and many others, are Goliaths in our midst.

Many of us are familiar with Jesus' instruction to His disciples: "The harvest is plentiful but the workers are few. Ask the Lord of the harvest, therefore, to send out workers into his harvest field" (Matt. 9:37–38). Immediately, Jesus sent out the very people He told to pray for workers! They were the answer to their own prayers. Since the day Jesus ascended to heaven from the hill outside Jerusalem, God has used His people to meet needs. We pray that God will work, and He does. He puts a burden on the hearts of those who love Him, He equips them to meet the need with specific talents and experiences, and then He launches them into the harvest field to love, share, lead, and care for broken, desperate people. We are the answer to people's prayers. We are the hands, feet, and voice of Jesus.

The needs of people aren't limited to a particular profile of race, gender, age, culture, nationality, or socioeconomic group. Everyone has deep psychological, social, physical, and spiritual needs. Some are more obvious than others. Each of us is uniquely anointed and appointed to meet a particular need. We often numb ourselves with entertainment. Instead, we need to let God inflame passionate unrest in our spirits that propels us to stand up and take action to meet the needs that have stirred our hearts. Let me put it this way: if you don't have a holy discontent, you're disconnected from the heart of God and the crying needs of people around you. Complacency isn't a fruit of the Spirit. Love notices, love cares, and love acts. We enjoy contentment because the Father and the Father's provision are more than enough to satisfy our souls. Divine joy frees us up to look outward and upward. When we are full, we can pour ourselves out into the lives of empty people around us.

YES AND NO

Once I asked my dad if I could go hang out at my friend Jermaine's house. This was a frequent request, and Jermaine and I were always at each other's home. Usually Dad had no reservations and would quickly say, "Sure, you can go." This time he reacted completely differently and almost strangely. He very slowly and reluctantly said, "No, this isn't a good day."

I spent quite a bit of time building up the courage to ask, "Why not?" I knew that was not a line of questioning my dad was fond of, and it would likely definitively close the door on my request. Nonetheless, I finally decided I had nothing to lose, so I began my barrage of interrogating questions in an effort to get him to change his answer. After all my pleas, his answer became an even more emphatic "Absolutely not." I felt that he was being mean, insensitive, unreasonable, and unfair—although I didn't let *any* of those thoughts leave my lips. That would have been a tragedy for sure.

About an hour later, he told my brothers and me to get ready to leave and headed toward the car. None of us knew what was going on or where we were going. By this time, I certainly wasn't going to risk asking, either. After about an hour's drive, I woke up to realize my dad had surprised us by taking us to our absolute favorite Mexican restaurant in the neighboring city. It was a major road trip to go, but always worth every minute of being stuck in the car. After indulging in a whole basket of pillow-shaped sopaipillas, I completely forgot my dad had denied my request to hang out with my friend Jermaine. His answer was a no to hanging out but a yes to enjoying my favorite restaurant. And the added bonus, unbeknownst to my brothers and me, my parents were taking us shopping for school clothes after we finished eating.

We can trust our wise and sovereign God to do what's best for us. When He says yes and opens a door, we can walk through it with confidence and gratitude. We realize this opportunity is the lane where we can serve God most effectively. Our passions give us energy; our talents make us useful. When we see lives changed, we give God all the credit.

But sometimes, God says, "Wait" or "No." These are tests of our faith. We need to look deeper than the present moment and realize the Lord of space and time has a plan for the ages. It's not His job to get on our wavelength. It's our task to get in tune with Him. He will get us out of any jam He has put us in. But if we've put ourselves there, we're on our own to get out!

If we insist on pushing our way through to make something happen when God has closed the door, we cause all kinds of problems. Of course, we need discernment to tell the difference between God's no and the Enemy's opposition. God's no may feel like the death of a dream, but it always comes with the promise of a resurrection. Something even better is around the corner. Or, God may be saying, "No, not yet. You need to work on your motives. I'm doing something wonderful you don't see yet." Either way, we trust that God always has good in mind—for us and for the people who are on our hearts. The Enemy often attacks us personally. He whispers in our ears that we're not good enough, God doesn't love us, or people will laugh at us. His three main tactics are temptation, accusation, and deception. Be on guard. Satan is crafty and cunning, and he wants to devour us.

Perhaps the bigger problem is when God says yes but we say no. At this crossroads, we become like Jonah, running from God and His calling and finding ourselves in the belly of a huge fish—a stinking, claustrophobic mess. If you want to end up in fish vomit, keep running from God! Keep your fingers in your ears to block out God's voice. When God points one way, go the other. Find excuses. Blame others. That's the way to guarantee a frustrated, angry, and depleted life.

No, that's not pretty, but it's the story of countless people who resisted God's summons and invitation to join Him in His great work of touching lives. The good news is that God is always waiting for us to respond. It's not too late until we're six feet under. Say yes today. It's the smart move. One of the beautiful things about God is that when we finally respond in faith, He usually opens doors very quickly. He's ready to pull the lever that opens the floodgates of blessing. He's just been waiting on us to reach out to Him. Even if obvious blessings don't happen immediately, something else does: we experience true contentment. When I finally stopped running from God's will and said yes to God's call to be a pastor, I gave up 80 percent of my income for several years. In return, God gave me something far more valuable: His peace. You can't buy that. It's a gift to His faithful children. I've been offered many opportunities to make a lot of money, but I've turned them down because they don't coincide with God's plan for me. No amount of money is worth living in the danger of being out of God's will.

THE PROCESS

At a conference for church leaders, Pastor T. D. Jakes said that the story of Moses illustrates a process God often uses to prepare us to trust Him and find our place of useful service. Moses had all the luxuries of the world when he lived in Pharaoh's palace, but those pleasures didn't fulfill him. When he recognized his true identity as a Hebrew, he left the wealth of the palace and humbled himself to be a slave, like his people. Time *with* the people gave him a heart *for* the people. His experience in the sweat of hard labor and the blood of the lash gave him empathy for those who labored next to him. When Moses saw a fellow slave being mistreated by an overseer, a fierce and holy discontent arose in him. He killed the Egyptian and fled into the desert to avoid execution. For forty long years Moses assumed his mission had failed and that God had forgotten him. Those were long, lonely years.

But God hadn't forgotten. During that time, God humbled Moses. Humility isn't weakness; it's power under control. When God told Moses to confront Pharaoh and demand freedom for the Hebrew slaves, Moses was reluctant—the opposite response from his impulsive reaction when he killed the Egyptian overseer years before. Here's the point: we're only truly qualified if we feel unqualified. Now, Moses was ready. God humbled him, equipped him with His calling and His power, and led Moses to stand *before* people—the Hebrew slaves, Pharaoh, and all the Egyptians—to represent almighty God.

With great courage, Moses, the dusty old shepherd who came back from the desert, confronted the most powerful ruler on earth. And the ruler blinked. After the ten plagues, Pharaoh finally let the people of God go free to the Promised Land. On the way to Palestine and their new homeland, God sent Moses up to Mount Sinai to receive the Ten Commandments, the law of God.

Moses had begun *outside* the people, stooped to be *with* the people, stood *before* the people, and finally, he was *above* the people as God's chosen representative. He was, as the Scripture says, the humblest man on earth. It took real humility and tenacious faith to face his own doubts, confront Pharaoh, and lead a bunch of malcontents across a searing desert to the place God had prepared for them. As much as any person who ever lived, Moses trusted God and tried God—and he found God to be trustworthy at every turn.

MAKE IT HAPPEN

When God puts a holy discontent in our hearts, we need to keep pushing and searching until we find a way to change the situation. When I was in high school, I wanted a car so bad I could taste it. I asked my father to buy me a car, but he wouldn't hear of it. It wasn't that he was a pastor on a limited salary. If he'd had all of Bill Gates's wealth, he still wouldn't have given me the money for a car. It was the principle of the thing. If I wanted a car, I had to earn the money.

For a long time, I shared a car with my mother—or rather, she shared her car with me. I dropped her off at work in the morning and picked her up in the afternoon. We had to coordinate our schedules so we both got where we needed to go. If the car had been cool, I'd have been fine with this arrangement. Cool it was not. It was a Chevy Eurosport. A *brown* Chevy Eurosport, with *brown* cloth seats. The hood was oxidized, but nobody could tell because it was just another shade of brown. Eventually, I was the only one who drove this car because my mother bought a brand-new Mitsubushi Diamante. I thought to myself, *Finally, I get my own ride.* But then the reality of the car's condition hit me again. After a while, the headliner in my newly adopted car sank down like a cloud around my head as I drove down the street. The loose foam falling from the ceiling made me look as though I had the worst case of orange dandruff the world had ever known.

I don't know how many times I asked my father to buy me a car, but his answer was always the same: "If I buy you a car, you won't appreciate it. You'll only value one if you earn the money and buy it yourself." I argued with him and tried to convince him that I'd treasure any car he'd buy for me (well, not just any car, but a nice one). I'd wash it, wax it, and keep it sparkling clean inside. Still, he wouldn't budge.

As time passed, I earned enough money to buy a car. I finally understood the principle my father had tried so hard to get through to me. If I really want something, I'll do whatever it takes to make it happen. This principle operates in every arena of life: in marriage, careers, health, friendships, sports—even our spiritual lives. It requires commitment, tenacity, and creativity. It pulls the best out of me, and it builds the best into me. When I've put everything into achieving or gaining a goal, I also have what it takes to maintain it and make it even better.

When we get things too easily (whether we're two or seventy-two), we don't sharpen our desires or develop our skills to use them properly. We can't *maintain* what we've *obtained.* As a result, the possessions become a weight we can't carry, and the blessing becomes a curse.

The measure of love isn't giving our spouses and kids everything they want. That's enabling, which then leads to a spirit of entitlement. We love people best by letting them desire something so much that it propels them to work, plan, and save until they can get it themselves. Then they'll appreciate it and pass the work ethic on to their children one day.

This is exactly how God treats His kids. He is the greatest giver, but He doesn't give us everything we want right away. Often, He gives us the desire, the resources, and the time to work hard to achieve our dreams. In the process, we learn life's most important lessons of value, honesty, endurance, and faith. As we develop those important muscles, we become qualified for even more responsibility.

A few years ago I decided I needed to get in shape, so I hired a trainer and began working out. After a month, I was still exhausted after every workout. One day, I complained that I hadn't made any progress at all. The trainer smiled and showed me a video of me lifting weights the first day, then showed me another video of the day before my complaint. The first one showed a deconditioned, out-of-shape guy who was fatigued after lifting a few pounds. The other one showed a guy with visibly developed muscles. I wondered, *Does this guy use Photoshop?* Then I realized it was really me!

I sent the video to my dad, and he had the same response. He called and said, "Who is that with all the muscles in his back? I know that's not you!"

I assured him it was.

He said, "You need to go see the doctor."

I answered, "What? What do you mean?"

He snapped back, "Because you're so full of it!"

That's my dad. Always a comedian, with an edge.

Muscles don't happen overnight—physically, spiritually, or in any other part of life. Muscles grow only when they face substantial resistance. Once they're broken down, they build back even stronger. If we're determined and consistent, amazing things can happen. We can gradually, almost imperceptibly, become much stronger day by day. Throughout the ages, people of great faith have told us that faith is always crafted in the hot forge of resistance. Adversity may be an unwelcome guest, but it's a magnificent trainer.

We sometimes think we need the power of the Spirit to accomplish great things. That's right; we do, but first, we need the strength of the Holy Spirit to be still and listen to God. How do you know when you're ready to trust God and take the lid off? The revelation comes when you surrender, endure His timing, and then listen to His no (when you want to hear yes) and be content in the realization that it is no longer about you. It is all about Him, His kingdom, and meeting the needs of those around you. When this is true of you, you're ready.

Our walks with God aren't passive. God is under no obligation to do everything for us. We do our part and God does His. It is a joint partnership. Paul explained it this way: "Therefore, my dear friends, as you have always obeyed—not only in my presence, but now much more in my absence—continue to work out your salvation with fear and trembling, for it is God who works in you to will and to act in order to fulfill his good purpose" (Phil. 2:12–13). We don't work *for* our salvation. Instead, we work hard because we're thrilled that we're *already* saved. And as we work, we trust God to lead us, empower us, and produce fruit in and through us.

TURTLE ON A FENCE

God has made us relational creatures. We are part of Christ's body. Too many of us live in a vacuum, believing we are on our own to walk with God and accomplish great things for Him. Little children go through a phase when they insist on doing things for themselves. When Carla and I would try to help our sons as toddlers, they would resist by saying, "I do it!" or "I got it." In wisdom, we would let them try things (most things, at least) until they got so frustrated they eventually called out for help. As adults, we need to learn the same lesson. We need one another. We're not the Lone Ranger. We look at famous, rich, and powerful individuals and mistakenly assume they got there on their own. Of course they didn't. Even the greatest entrepreneurs, political leaders, musicians, and movie stars are products of others who poured insight, energy, time, and training into them at critical times in their lives. If they need it, you and I need it too.

Not long ago, I saw a picture of a turtle on a fence post. The caption under it read, "I didn't get here by myself." Being a keen observer of nature, I realized, "Turtles can't climb." They're heavy, slow, and awkward, even on level ground. Someone had to put that turtle high on the fence post.

For the turtle, for me, and for everyone else, building a team of dedicated people is one of the most important things we can do to take the lid off. With them, we have far more energy, creativity, productivity, and fun. Without them, we soon burn out because we work too hard, or we give up and quit because we lose the joy and feel burnout set in.

We have formal teams at work and in organizations, but we also have informal teams in our families and friendships. Every person who is close to us is part of our team. They contribute to our success, and we contribute to theirs. In fact, we may have different teams for different aspects of our lives. I have a team to lead our church, a team for my music endeavors, a team to help publish my books, a team of mentors who help me grow spiritually and in my leadership skills, and my family "team" who keeps me grounded and makes life worthwhile.

When we say yes to God, we experience supernatural peace and power. It is amazing that God uses people like us to comfort those who are hurting, to give direction to people who are confused, and to provide resources for those in need. Every week when I stand in the pulpit, I'm amazed when I see God transforming lives by using the Word He has given to me to preach. I'm also amazed at the countless acts of kindness and love expressed by our people in their homes, businesses, schools, and neighborhoods. In every place and in every way, God has chosen to use ordinary people to do extraordinary things.

Sometimes, I'm awestruck with the thought, *God, I matter enough to You for You to use me. I'm important enough to You for You to take me in Your hand and mold me into an instrument of Your glory!* That's what He's doing with everyone who truly follows Him—and it's amazing.

In summary, don't be surprised when you find your heart

troubled by the needs of others. Holy discontent is a sure sign the Spirit of God is at work to give you the heart of Christ. Listen carefully, get your instructions from God, and then trust Him by taking bold steps of faith. Along the way, you'll encounter resistance. When you trust God to do great things, you'll try Him and find Him faithful. But He'll also put you through trials. Don't panic. It's normal. Be strong, be determined, and exercise your spiritual muscles. From first to last, draw people around you and build a team of mutual support and encouragement.

Get ready. You're in for the ride of your life!

> My own weaknesses make me shrink, but God's promises make me brave.
>
> —CHARLES HADDON SPURGEON

CONSIDER THESE QUESTIONS

1. What are some examples of holy discontent? What are your personal examples? What are you doing about it?
2. Read 1 Samuel 17. Describe David's motivation, resources, opposition, threats, and action. What are some Goliaths in your world? What would it look like for you to be a David in these situations?
3. How do trials qualify you and prepare your heart?
4. How can you tell whether God is saying no or the Enemy is trying to discourage you? What are some principles that define the difference?
5. What are some ways God is giving you opportunities to

build your spiritual muscles? Are you receptive to this training? Explain your answer.

6. Describe your team and the impact you have on one another. Do any changes need to be made? If so, what are they?

PART 4

ONWARD

SEVEN

SEE IT, SAY IT, SENSE IT, SEEK IT

I have been impressed with the urgency of doing. Knowing is not enough; we must apply. Being willing is not enough, we must do.

—LEONARDO DA VINCI

SOMETIMES GOD'S BLESSINGS COME SO BIG AND FAST THAT THEY THREATEN TO overwhelm us! If we're not careful, the flood of the Spirit's power can swamp our boat. That's what happened to me. Not long after we started the church, crowds of people came to be touched by the Lord's message of goodness and hope. Soon, more than two thousand people came through our doors every Sunday. This was glorious, but initially it presented enormous challenges. I'd watched my father lead churches of five hundred members, but I had never seen anyone lead a church like the one we were building. In the beginning, I was the person responsible for everything, from greeting people when they walked in the doors in the morning, to saying good-bye when they left after the service. I was in charge of the music, the offering, the administration, and leadership development. Every decision came to my desk, and I couldn't handle it all—I became a bottleneck. God was doing amazing things, but I was exhausted! I became frustrated and impatient, and the people serving in our church became frustrated and impatient with me. (It was equal-opportunity stress!)

One day I poured out my discouragement to a friend who was also a local pastor. He listened to me talk about my misery, and as I mentioned at the beginning of the book, he offered a ray of hope. He told me about a leadership expert who had helped him in incredible ways. To say the least, I was very interested. He explained that this man, Dr. Samuel Chand, had helped him institute systems that enabled his church to run far more smoothly. And even better, the systems freed him to do what he does best: teach, preach, and lead.

A few weeks later, Dr. Chand, Carla, and I had dinner together at his favorite steak house, Morton's. I explained my predicament and shared my frustration. After a few minutes, Dr. Chand began drawing on a napkin. A few minutes later, he turned it around and pushed it across the table. "I think this is what you're missing," he said with a smile.

It was a simple and workable organizational chart. As he explained it, I felt as ignorant as a little boy looking at the diagrams for the space shuttle, but Dr. Chand made it all crystal clear. I wondered, *Why haven't I already seen this? How did I miss this?*

My problem wasn't that I didn't have a strategy. I had one, but it didn't fit the requirements of the situation. When it didn't work, I just tried it with more intensity (and blamed others for not trying as hard as I did). On the napkin, Dr. Chand showed me a different strategy—one that fit the needs of my circumstances. I didn't need a strategy; I needed *the right* strategy.

The new strategy was to empower others to own aspects of our ministry. My role was to give them direction, involve them in the decision-making process, and then give them the authority to carry out the ministry entrusted to them. I no longer had to do everything; therefore, I felt relieved. Likewise, the leaders in our church felt the freedom and joy of serving with all their hearts. It worked for all of us—with plenty of minor adjustments along the way.

Dr. Chand helped me realize we were trying to do too many things, which diluted the vision of the church and the passion of our people. He kept asking me, "What's the one thing God has called you to do?" For a while, I had a hard time digging down past the hundred good things and the dozen really good things to find the one central calling God had given me. Finally, I got there. Our church uses the acronym LEAD: learning, empowering, assigning, and developing.

I realized that many people stand on the sidelines and watch, but you can't coach people until they get in the game. God wanted us to assign people to particular roles in our church and our community. This would get them involved, enlist their talents, and bring out the best in them. I knew that once they saw God use them to change lives, they would get excited and enlist even more people to join us. The leadership strategy I enlisted in our church was a success. We watched as the snowball effect of the Spirit's love and power grew larger and stronger!

A vision isn't enough, though. A workable strategy is necessary to get from point A to point B. But a strategy isn't much help unless there is something worthwhile to aim for. Every person, every company, and every organization needs both: (1) a clear and compelling vision and (2) an effective tailored strategy. When we read the historical record of the Scriptures, we find men and women who succeeded when they had a vision-driven strategy. For example, Moses had a vision for freeing the children of God from slavery in Egypt and leading them to the Promised Land. He implemented a detailed strategy, adapting it as needed, to face every opposition and obstacle.

To turn a vision into reality, we need to go through a simple and profound process: see it, say it, sense it, and seek it.

SEE IT

There are, I believe, two kinds of minds: creative and strategic. Both types have particular burdens and blessings. Creative people have the phenomenal ability to see the unseen. Artists have a vision of the painting or sculpture before they pick up the brush or hold the lump of clay in their hands. Creative leaders envision the success of an endeavor before they've taken the first step. Creative people are the lifeblood of any organization, but they can also suck the life out of people because they often fail to combine their wonderful vision with a workable strategy. They get the cart before the horse—and they may not even know they need a horse!

When I taught high school, I had some students who were always living in another world. They were dreamers. That's fantastic, but they needed to learn how to anchor their dreams to planet Earth! They were looking at their pagers (remember those?), writing notes, and daydreaming during class. When I'd finish a lecture to the class, many would raise their hands and say, "Mr. Norful, I don't understand what you want us to do. Would you explain it to me?" Their failure to pay attention frustrated me and cost the class valuable time. I reminded all my students to give me their undivided attention, but I had to remind the dreamers more often. I told them to FOCUS: Find Our Center of Understanding Systems. If they weren't prepared, the reality of the next test would crash into their mental wonderland.

Creative people may be distracted from the task at hand, but they're always thinking, considering, and imagining a better future. Creative people push past the barriers to grasp the impossible. They refuse to take no for an answer. The future is almost tangible in their minds. The writer to the Hebrews explained that all of us need this kind of vision and faith: "And without faith it is impossible to please God, because anyone who comes to him must believe that he exists and that he rewards those who earnestly seek him" (Heb. 11:6). The world, the church, and our families are richer and brighter because creative people infuse new possibilities into our lives. They have ideas that can transform the world, but only if these ideas find meaningful expressions in reality. It's not enough to have the most phenomenal cart in the history of humankind. We need a horse to take it somewhere! Systems are the horse, the strategy, the plan, and the implementation steps to fulfill the vision.

Some people, though, are all horse and no cart. They're very detailed and use repeatable systems to keep everything organized, but they're sometimes so focused on working the system that they forget it's supposed to help them do something magnificent! Many people are very detailed in their thinking, planning, and implementation. Excellence is a virtue, but perfectionism is a problem. (You might even call some of them "rigid," but we won't mention any names.) Dreamers see the possibilities; critical perfectionists focus on the problems. They have a million reasons why something won't work, why it can't succeed, and why people won't buy it. Their negativity drains the faith and hope out of everyone around them.

Quite often, the doubters are right—but they're only half-right. They may have accurately identified the difficulties, but they haven't identified the creative solutions to overcome those problems. We need to see the challenges, but we also need to have a vision for the potential success of any event or venture.

When strategic thinkers blend their natural ability with a good dose of optimism, amazing things can happen. They see all the details that need to be addressed, but they don't get bogged down. They keep the vision in front of them, clear away the debris of doubts, and find a way to accomplish something wonderful.

Are you a cart person or a horse person? Are you a dreamer who needs to value systems and details, or are you an analytical person who needs to keep the vision fresh and alive? Every church, every family, every business, and every neighborhood has both kinds of people. In fact, opposites attract, so many couples exemplify the beauty of these two working together and the strife when they don't.

If you typically fill the cart with all kinds of creative ideas, learn to appreciate the horse that can pull you into reality. If you have a strong horse, remember that it's designed to pull something. Vision *and* strategy—both are essential if we're going to see clearly into the future.

When I started the church, a dear lady told me that she really appreciated my vision and tenacity. She explained, "Most people start with 'Ready . . . get set,' but they never 'go.' Pastor, you're 'go, get set, and ready.'" She, like Dr. Chand, realized I needed a strategy to help me fulfill my creative vision. I've learned some important lessons from these people who told me the truth.

SAY IT

If an idea stays in our heads, it may not have enough clarity or energy to become real. Two activities accomplish wonders in the planning process: speaking and writing. When we talk about our plans, they take shape, we affirm them as our own, and we invite feedback from others. The process of writing our ideas takes this process one step further. Writing forces us to consider every word—the connection of thoughts and the implications of our concepts.

The prophet Habakkuk lived in a time of unprecedented calamity. The nation of Israel had experienced a cultural and economic collapse. In the middle of the suffering, the prophet "stationed himself in the tower" to hear from God. Into the darkness, God sent the light of instruction and hope. Someday, God would accomplish more than Habakkuk (or anyone else) could imagine. To make it plain and clear for then and for all time, God told him to put pen to paper:

> Then the LORD replied: "Write down the revelation and make it plain on tablets so that a herald may run with it. For the revelation awaits an appointed time; it speaks of the end and will not prove false. Though it linger, wait for it; it will certainly come and will not delay." (Hab. 2:2–3)

As long as our hopes and dreams remain stuck between our ears, we don't take steps to accomplish them. When we don't say or write our vision and strategic plans, we limit our faith and shortchange our potential. The process of talking, listening, shaping, writing, and crafting our plans invites us into God's boardroom to think His thoughts and dream His dreams, but it also puts us on the production floor to chart out the specific steps needed to fulfill the dream. Speaking and writing put our faith out on the table to be examined, nurtured, corrected, and inflamed.

When I spoke on this topic in our church, I told our people, "God has put a dream in your heart, but many of you have been denying it, ignoring it, and rejecting it—out of fear. You're afraid of failing. You're afraid of looking like a fool." I told them to turn to the person next to them—a spouse, a friend, or a total stranger—and tell that person the dream God had put on their hearts. Speak it out loud, infuse it with the honor and power of the spoken word, and trust God to make it a reality. When they did this, many people felt uncomfortable, but they found the courage to verbalize a dream God had put in their hearts. Many had been carrying their dreams for years, but until that moment, even those closest to them had no idea it was even there.

Visionaries need to verbalize their dreams as well as their strategies. Analysts need to verbalize their compelling hopes as well as their detailed plans. Cart and horse—both are important as we verbalize and write the vision.

Many people assume their dreams are just crazy ideas that are somehow divorced from their relationship with God. To be sure, some of our ideas aren't from God, but many are. God speaks His vision into our hearts. Then we find the courage to verbalize it to those we trust. They may push back to challenge our thinking. That's good and right, but don't let a doubting perfectionist ruin your dream! Find people who have a beautiful blend of vision and strategic thinking. Those are the people whose advice is most valuable.

Of course, when we think about the power of the written word, we realize we already have God's Word in the Scriptures. God gave Moses the written law on Mount Sinai, and the prophets wrote down God's Word to His people. When Satan tempted Jesus in the wilderness—when the Enemy tried to put the lid on Him—He responded, "It is written . . ." When the Pharisees opposed Him, Jesus responded with the written Word. If Jesus needed the written Word of God to stand strong and accomplish all that the Father called Him to do, how much more do we need it? Our vision, then, needs to be in line with the purposes and the heart of God. How do we know? By reading and studying the Bible and letting God's Word sink deep into our souls.

Articulating the vision and strategy makes it *clear* to us and to those around us, it makes the plans *concrete* and *concise,* and it gives our message *consistency.* It takes time and effort, but it pays huge dividends.

SENSE IT

The default mode of the human heart is selfishness. It's the direction we drift when we're not watching our hearts' condition, and it's the pit we fall into when we let our sinful desires run rampant. One of the marks of a mature believer is a heart that's sensitive to the Spirit of God. When I've seen people do things for selfish motives, they may begin with enthusiasm, but they end up miserable. And they have very little impact for God's kingdom.

To fulfill God's assignment for our lives, we need to sense God's pleasure, His will, and His path. We sense His pleasure when we realize it's all about grace. We are so sinful it took the death of the Son of God to pay for our sins, but He loves us so much He was glad to die for us. God doesn't just tolerate His children. He loves us with the tender, fierce love of a mother grizzly! We perform out of our identity as chosen, adopted, forgiven children of the King. We don't get our identity by performing to earn His approval. This is crucial, but many Christians miss it. Paul put it this way, "For Christ's love compels us, because we are convinced that one died for all, and therefore all died. And he died for all, that those who live should no longer live for themselves but for him who died for them and was raised again" (2 Cor. 5:14–15). We don't negotiate deals with God to get Him to bless us. And we don't expect God to be a doting grandfather who is senile and generous. God is the King of glory, and we are His beloved sons and daughters. Everything we do comes out of the wonder of this magnificent identity, and it's all based on His marvelous grace. When we sense the wonder of His love, we want to honor Him more than anything. Then, and only then, are we ready to pursue His will and His path.

It's important to remember that our choices are a product of our identity as beloved, forgiven, empowered children of the King. Many people get this backward: they try to prove themselves by what they do. When they perform well and earn accolades, they feel euphoric and powerful—and prideful. But when they fail, they either collapse in despair or try even harder to prove themselves. A compelling, strong foundation makes all the difference in our motivations and our choices. No matter what line of work we're in—from a stay-at-home mom to a corporate CEO to a pastor—God has given us a kingdom assignment. No matter where we serve, we represent the King and Savior.

When I graduated from college, I became the American civics teacher at Jack Robey Junior High School in Pine Bluff, Arkansas. Only a few years before, I'd been a student in the school, and many of the teachers who had taught me were still there. I was so excited! The transition, though, wasn't always smooth. On the first day, I walked into the teachers' lounge, and one of my former teachers recognized me. She barked, "What are you doing in here? This is the teachers' lounge, and you're not supposed to be in here!"

I calmly replied, "I'm a new teacher here now."

She threw her head back and said, loudly, "Oh, Lord, it's time for me to retire!"

People laughed, but I realized an important point. If I lived according to my God-given assignment, I'd walk in confidence and humility. But if I was afraid of ridicule, I'd constantly be trying to prove myself, hide my insecurities, and jockey for praise.

Every day in the lounge, I listened to teachers I'd admired and feared when I was a boy. Behind the closed doors, I heard them gripe about the administration and complain about the students. I rarely heard a positive comment. In fact, they seemed to compete in telling the most awful stories about the kids in their classrooms. I couldn't relate. I was having a blast in my classroom every day. I loved teaching the kids, and they were excited about all they were learning. When I walked through the door of the teachers' lounge, it felt as if I were walking into a foreign country that had no connection to my experiences in class each day.

About halfway through the school year, I was sitting in a departmental meeting. The smaller group had somehow intensified their complaints. They talked about how they hated their jobs, how unfair the system was, and how their students were driving them crazy. I'd been quiet a long time, but my holy discontent overflowed at that moment. I was still very calm and measured, but I interrupted the gripe-fest and said, "Excuse me. Can I ask a question?" Every eye turned to me. "Is this what you should be doing?"

At first, some of them assumed I was asking about the necessity of having a departmental meeting. I explained, "It appears none of you are happy and fulfilled as teachers. I'm wondering if being a teacher is what you should be doing with your lives and your careers?"

I hadn't meant for my observations and question to be offensive. But the teachers were furious and offended. One of the teachers spoke for the others. She glared at me and said, "How dare you?

You've only been here a few months, and you think you have the right to criticize us?"

I didn't back down. I nodded to acknowledge her right to speak her opinion, but I continued. "Yes, I'm new, but not that new anymore. I've listened to all of you for almost four months, and the pattern is very clear. You have very few positive things to say—about anything or anyone. I'm amazed that so many teachers are obviously miserable in their jobs. I wonder if this is really the vocation for those who are so unhappy every day. I know it's what I'm supposed to be doing. I enjoy teaching. I love the kids, and I see enormous potential in them. I face challenges, and I need help to overcome them. But I'm sure I can make a difference in my students' lives. Every day, I'm filled with joy and hope in my classroom. But I don't see that in you. You all don't seem to be looking for solutions. Instead, the majority of the teachers here are wallowing in the problems."

That day, I sensed my calling and God's direction to calmly and lovingly speak truth into a difficult situation. I'd like to say that all the people thanked me and said how God had used me to change their attitudes, but that didn't happen. From that day on, I had a very large target on my back. When I walked into the teachers' lounge, they treated me as if I had swine flu, leprosy, and bubonic plague all wrapped into one! I didn't have to wonder about bumping into anyone, because they all quickly scattered to stay away from me. My job, though, was never in jeopardy. As God would have it, my father was the president of the local school board. In the words of Bishop Jakes, "Favor ain't fair."

All of us need God to give us a kingdom assignment. It may change over time, but at each stage of our lives, we need to know we're right in the middle of God's will for us. There are, of course, no guarantees that following God's perfect will makes things smooth and easy. Just look at Jesus. No one ever followed the Father's will as perfectly, but it led Him into ridicule, rejection, misunderstanding, betrayal, torture, and death. Few of us will ever face anything remotely similar to this kind of heartache for following Christ, but God's path leads us into valleys as surely as He takes us to mountaintops. When we're convinced God has given us an assignment, we don't wallow in self-pity or blame others when things don't go well. Instead, we realize God has given us a wonderful opportunity to trust Him—an opportunity that's cleverly disguised as an insurmountable problem. With this faith-filled perspective, difficult people and situations become stepping-stones to growth instead of roadblocks.

Finding the right fit in a vocation isn't easy. In fact, it's relatively rare. A Gallup poll showed that only 30 percent of American workers enjoy their jobs. The report indicates that 20 percent are "actively disengaged." These people regularly complain about their work, their managers, and their colleagues. They try to get out of responsibilities, and they may use lunch breaks to look for other job openings. Fully 50 percent of Americans in the workforce are "disengaged." They do their work, but without joy, passion, and a sense of being part of something bigger than themselves.[1] Sadly, many of the people responding to the survey are undoubtedly Christians. They live each day with a deep, pervasive sense that their lives don't count. It's tragic, but it's correctable.

I meet people all the time who can't stand what they do each day. I don't make fun of them because I've been there too. One of the jobs I had after college was being a National Park Service ranger at the Blue Ridge Parkway in Asheville, North Carolina. I gave presentations to park visitors, chased bears out of campsites, and wandered in the woods to check on trails after heavy rains. I know some Boy Scouts who would love this job, but I hated it. The scenery was beautiful, the people were pleasant, but it didn't work for me. I had to leave and find something that fit my talents and my passions.

For a variety of reasons, many people feel stuck in dead-end jobs. Some are afraid to try something new. The paycheck they receive is more attractive than the adventure of launching into something unknown. Others don't want to take the risk of uprooting their families. However, they don't realize the damage they're doing to their kids as they watch their parents grumble, complain, and despise their work every day. Some complain that they don't have the degree or certification for the career they want. Or they look to family and friends as the source of their income and stability. They don't realize there's a far greater Source who delights in meeting the needs of those who trust Him.

Years ago I heard an illustration that perfectly fits the condition of the 70 percent of people who hate their unfulfilling jobs. A young eagle is put into a pen full of chickens. As the eagle grows, he has all the potential in the world, but his culture communicates that all he can ever be is a chicken. He grows strong wings and sharp talons, but he never uses them. Every day, the farmer tries to get the eagle to take off and fly, but he refuses. His self-image is a reflection of the chickens all around him. He doesn't sense his real identity, so he never lives according to it—he never takes flight.

Another example is when I took my children to the circus. In the ring, a man led a huge, powerful elephant by a slim rope. In the wild, elephants knock down trees; swim rivers, using their trunks as snorkels; and are the intimidating rulers of their domains. But the elephant in the circus had lost sight of his power and majesty. It had become a docile pet. Many people today are like the eagle or the elephant. They have incredible talents and power, but they live powerless, meaningless, boring lives. It doesn't have to stay that way.

One of the most important questions we ask ourselves is, who am I? The question that follows is, to whom do I belong? If we are Christians, we have been delivered from the domain of darkness and transferred into the kingdom of God. We were once enemies of God, but now we are His beloved sons and daughters. We were once outcasts; now He has brought us near and seated us at His banquet table. We were once weak and helpless; now the power of the Holy Spirit lives in each of us. We were once lost in selfishness and emptiness; now God has entrusted us to redeem a lost and dying world so we all might experience His grace, love, and strength. Everything we have is a gift from the hand of a loving Father, and we have the unutterable privilege of joining hands with Him to fulfill His divine destiny on earth and for all eternity.

Do you sense it? Do you feel the high honor and the deep humility of this identity? It's all yours, and no one can take it away from you. You are not what your past, your family, your friends, or your failures say about you. You are more than that. You are God's. You are the heir, not the forgotten one. You are rich in grace, no longer a pauper. You are more than a conqueror; you are a victor. You are a new creation, bought with the blood of Jesus and seated with Him in glory at the right hand of the Father.

The psalmist said, "Taste and see that the Lord is good" (Ps. 34:8). We may have been told that honey is sweet, and we may have read about its sweetness. But we don't truly know the sweetness of honey until we dip our spoons in it and taste it. Many people in our churches, homes, and businesses can speak the truth of right doctrine about the goodness and grace of God, but to many of them, it's still just an abstract theory. They haven't tasted God's goodness. They haven't marveled at the wonder of His delicious, nourishing, satisfying love. Sensing God's grace and purpose is more than intellectual knowledge of it. It begins with this kind of knowledge, but it must move past the mind and into the depths of our hearts. When we sense it there, everything changes.

Some people may shake their heads and say, "Well, I'm not so sure. I don't think God has done enough to convince me." Not enough? That's the complaint of fearful, lethargic people through the ages. In the desert, the children of Israel complained to Moses and wanted to go back to slavery in Egypt. Hadn't God proven Himself to them? He had sent plagues, set them free, parted the Red Sea to let them cross on dry ground, and made this door of freedom a trap for Pharaoh's army. He provided water, manna, and quail for them. God gave them His laws to guide them and the tabernacle and sacrifices to forgive them. And they didn't think it was enough. And how about Jesus' disciples? They had been eyewitnesses of miracles, healings, incredible teaching, and His transfigured glory, and Jesus had saved their lives when He stilled the storm. They'd had a front-row seat, but they ran scared when the soldiers came to arrest Him. The task for us is the same as it has been in all generations. Our natural inclination is to doubt God's goodness and power. We need to rivet our minds on the truth of God, sense His greatness and grace, and trust Him to lead us.

King Solomon observed, "For as he thinks in his heart, so *is* he" (Prov. 23:7 NKJV). Step back and notice how you think—about God, yourself, your circumstances, and your future. Change your thinking and change your life. If we sense our powerful, dynamic, secure identity in Christ, we'll have the courage and passion to take the lid off and follow Him anywhere He leads us.

SEEK IT

An Indy race car can have a thousand horsepower of potential, but until the driver puts it in gear and pushes on the gas, it stays immobile. God has given us phenomenal potential, but we have to take action to turn potential into a powerful reality. James reminds us, "Faith by itself, if it is not accompanied by action, is dead" (James 2:17). Look at it this way: true faith always moves people to action. If it doesn't, it's just an idea, an empty hope, a powerless concept. In a parallel passage, Paul tells us, "For God did not give us a spirit of timidity, but a spirit of power, of love and of self-discipline" (2 Tim. 1:7 NIV 1984).

Timidity comes in many forms. Many people are afraid of failure, but some are also terrified of success because they don't think they can live up to it very long. They may be afraid of the unknown, and they don't have a stomach for the risks involved. Too often, people look inside at their own resources and wisdom—or lack of them—and they shudder. Instead, we need to look to the limitless resources of God and find the courage to take the next step in the journey of discovery. Without faith, we're destined to stay stuck in neutral. But with faith, all things are possible.

When we read the Psalms, we realize that many of them aren't prayers, and they aren't songs. Sometimes the writer isn't talking to God, and he isn't teaching a group of believers. He's talking to himself. One of them says, "Find rest, O my soul, in God alone; my hope comes from him. He alone is my rock and my salvation; he is my fortress, I will not be shaken. My salvation and my honor depend on God; he is my mighty rock, my refuge" (Ps. 62:5–7 NIV 1984). The psalmist is telling himself the truth about God. Then, with a new sense of confidence, he prays, "One thing God has spoken, two things have I heard: that you, O God, are strong, and that you, O Lord, are loving. Surely you will reward each person according to what he has done" (vv. 11–12 NIV 1984). Like the psalmist, we often need to give ourselves a pep talk so our faith is propelled into action.

If we're natural visionaries, we need to take time to develop a workable strategy. If we're analytical and cautious, we need a fresh injection of hope that a venture will make a difference. We may come from different points, but sooner or later, we need to take action. The first step may be bold, or it may be halting. The important thing is to take the step regardless of the outcome. There are no guarantees. Almost always, we'll make mistakes, but we can learn from them. We'll make midcourse corrections and keep moving forward.

Sometimes, the initiative isn't ours. Circumstances force us to make a move. A tragic accident, betrayal by someone we love, or a new door of opportunity comes when we least expect it. In every case, we have choices to make. Whether we initiate the choice or it's thrust upon us, we can respond with careful thinking, courageous faith, and clear steps forward.

Up to this moment, we have been identifying the lid and putting our hands on it. Now we take the lid off and see what God will do in and through us. These are the most challenging and thrilling moments in our lives!

I've heard that the richest field of dreams in the world is a cemetery. Countless people lived with great hopes and plans but never acted on them. When they died, their dreams died with them. Cures for cancer, transformed families, new products, great organizations, and tender mercies are buried six feet under. Don't be mistaken: God will accomplish His purposes with or without us. His divine plan will be fulfilled, but we have a choice: will we be His partners, or will we stand on the sidelines?

When we see it, say it, sense it, and seek it, the process will be messy—don't be surprised at the fiery trials you experience—but it will be glorious. These four elements are always part of God's design for His children. When we follow His path, we'll be touched by His heart and led by His Spirit. When you follow this path, you'll be in alignment with His purposes and His power. God is waiting for you to join Him. Don't miss it.

> Never forget that you are one of a kind. Never forget that if there weren't any need for you in all your uniqueness to be on this earth, you wouldn't be here in the first place. And never forget, no matter how overwhelming life's challenges and problems seem to be, that one person can make a difference in the world. In fact, it is always because of one person that all the changes that matter in the world come about. So be that one person.
>
> —RICHARD BUCKMINSTER FULLER

CONSIDER THESE QUESTIONS

1. Are you a person with a creative mind or someone with a strategic mind? What are the strengths of your approach? What are some limitations and liabilities?
2. What are some specific steps you can take to be more balanced and comprehensive? For example, if you're creative, whose strategic input do you need to consider?
3. How do speaking and writing a vision make it clearer and more powerful?
4. What has God been saying to you (in the last few years,

the last few weeks, or as you read this chapter) about the direction He wants you to go? Write it down, and tell somebody today.

5. What are some differences between intellectually knowing something is true and tasting its truth? What are you sensing from God?
6. What is the next step for you to find and follow God's dream for your life? When and how will you take it? Who will give you the support you need as you take this step?

EIGHT

DREAM AGAIN

We cannot change our past. We cannot change the fact that people act in a certain way. We cannot change the inevitable. The only thing we can do is play on the one string we have, and that is our attitude.

—CHARLES R. SWINDOLL

AT A CRUCIAL MOMENT IN MY LIFE, I WONDERED, *IS THIS ALL THERE IS?*

From the time I was a little boy, my dream was to become a recording artist. At every opportunity, I volunteered to sing—at church, in school, at home, in the car, maybe even in my sleep. As I grew up, my hopes became even more focused. I saw people I admired winning national awards, and I worked hard to get to that level of excellence. I devoted every ounce of energy and every second of time to do my best. I climbed over rocks of adversity, and I struggled up broken ladders on my way up. The acclaim began to come, and in fact, I received far more awards than I'd ever dreamed of winning. The favor of God was resting on me in a magnificent way. Then, one day I took a deep breath and looked at my life. I had accomplished my goals and fulfilled my dreams, but I felt strangely empty. I wondered, *Is this all there is? Where's the rest? There's got to be more to life than this.*

Everything that had happened to me was right in the center

of God's favor, timing, purpose, and will. It took some time for me to realize it, but I discovered that dreams aren't static. They grow, they change, and they develop. God has made us so that even the greatest accomplishments can't fill the gaping hole in our souls. The brilliant philosopher, theologian, and mathematician Blaise Pascal, observed, "There is a God-shaped vacuum in the heart of every person, and it can never be filled by any created thing. It can only be filled by God, made known through Jesus Christ."

ALWAYS MORE

All around us, people are trying to force limited dreams into the vacuum that only God can fill. New England Patriots quarterback Tom Brady is one of the greatest players the NFL has ever known. He led his team to five Super Bowl wins and was four times voted the National Football Leagues' MVP (Most Valuable Player). He has a supermodel wife, makes tens of millions each year from his NFL contract and endorsements, and his teammates love him because he honors them every chance he gets. No one, it seems, has more of the good life than Tom Brady.

But it's not enough. In an interview with Steve Kroft of *60 Minutes* in 2005, he complained that in spite of all the money, success, and acclaim, he still felt confused and empty. He mused, "Why do I have three Super Bowl rings, and still think there's something greater out there for me?" He had reached his highest goals and fulfilled every desire, but he complained sadly, "God, it's gotta be more than this!"

Kroft asked, "What's the answer?"

Brady laughed. "I wish I knew. . . . I love playing football, and I love being a quarterback for this team, but at the same time, I think there's a lot of other parts about me that I'm trying to find."[1]

If fulfilling his dreams ultimately left Tom Brady feeling empty, it's foolish to think fulfilling ours will truly satisfy us. No matter how much money, fame, and pleasure we enjoy, God always has more for us. We can enjoy success for a moment, but we have to remember that it's just a gift. The Giver is far more important, more powerful, and more satisfying. And He always has even bigger dreams for us.

When I meet someone who is confused because he or she has accomplished wonderful goals but still feels empty, I've learned to ask, "When was the last time you dreamed?" Those who hear this question from me often smile and shake their heads just before giving a myriad of excuses for staying stuck in the good instead of striving again for the best. They point to their ages, their limited resources, their family situations, and a dozen other reasonable hindrances. Soon, the deadening monotony of life settles like concrete around these folks' lives—and it feels completely normal to settle for a dull, meaningless life. Yes, all of these reasons are very real, but we need to remember that our God is far greater than any obstacle. He can move mountains—even mountains of doubt.

If anyone had reason to make excuses, it was the apostle Paul. He had given everything to the cause of Christ. He traveled from city to city, knowing he would be beaten, whipped, and imprisoned. At dozens of points, he could have said, "That's enough! God, I've done plenty for You. I've planted churches. I've written letters to nearly a dozen churches. I've walked a thousand miles, and I'm tired. It's time for me to retire. I want to find a little fishing village and hide the rest of my life. No more risk, no more threats, no more suffering. I'm done!"

But Paul never said that. In fact, he always dreamed of seeing God use him even more powerfully. From jail, he wrote to the Philippians that suffering didn't compare to "the surpassing greatness of knowing Christ Jesus my Lord" (Phil. 3:8 NIV 1984). Then he explained that he, the greatest leader the church has ever known, wasn't satisfied or complacent. He wrote:

> Not that I have already obtained all this, or have already been made perfect, but I press on to take hold of that for which Christ Jesus took hold of me. Brothers, I do not consider myself yet to have taken hold of it. But one thing I do: Forgetting what is behind and straining toward what is ahead, I press on toward the goal to win the prize for which God has called me heavenward in Christ Jesus. All of us who are mature should take such a view of things." (Phil. 3:12–15 NIV 1984)

As we walk with Jesus, we'll be thrilled to see His blessings and power displayed through us. But we will know there's always something more for us to do for Him. Like Jesus and His disciples, we may take retreats to rest and be restored, but we come back to "strain toward what is ahead," "pressing on toward" the new vision, expecting to "win the prize" that waits for us in Christ.

Many people are consumed with what happened in the past. Some look back and complain, and others look back with satisfaction. The point, though, is that they're always looking backward. When all you talk about is yesterday, you've stopped growing, you've stopped pressing onward, and you've stopped dreaming. If there's nothing in the future that challenges you and brings out the best in you, you'll become stagnant. You'll stop growing, and all your talents will wither.

The American dream is to retire well and retire early. Paul's attitude (and ours, if we understand God's calling in our lives) is that we never retire from our ultimate dream of knowing, loving, and serving Jesus Christ. Our goal isn't to get to a place where there are no longer any challenges. When life has no challenges, it also has no meaning. Our goal is to keep reaching, keep stretching, keep knocking, and keep trusting God to use us in even bigger ways—until our last breath. I'm not suggesting that we keep doing the same things all our lives. We may retire from a particular role at work, but we never retire from our God-inspired, Spirit-driven pursuit of extending the kingdom of God to every person we meet.

I've talked to a wide spectrum of people who are trying to reach a certain point, and when they get there, they assume they can coast for the rest of their lives. Young parents may focus their goals on the point when their last child is out of diapers. Others look forward to the time their kids leave home after high school, when they graduate from college, or when their last child is married. Many others have their sights set on a certain income level, a coveted position at work, or a particular amount in their retirement account. All of these are good benchmarks, but they aren't the ultimate fulfillment of God's design for the lives of His children.

When people are young, their vision often drifts toward self-focused goals of making a comfortable living, finding a beautiful or handsome spouse, and moving up the corporate ladder. There's nothing wrong with these things if we see them as gifts from God and He remains in the center of our affections and ambitions. But when our dreams are misplaced, we ruin the gifts God has given us.

When people are older, they often assume they've earned the right to sit back and watch as others do all the work. They may not have the physical stamina and strength they had when they were young, but they have a wealth of experience and wisdom to share with others. Everything they are, everything they have, and every relationship can be used to honor Him. I've seen desperate needs in churches and communities that remained unmet because young people assumed older generations would take responsibility, and older people sat on their hands because they'd concluded they'd done enough for God in past years. In every family, every church, and every community, evil is flourishing and people are desperate for someone—anyone—to stand in the gap. God has prepared each person with lavish amounts of time, talents, resources, and experiences. We can't let God's gifts go to waste! There are too many crushing needs around us for the people of God to stand on the sidelines.

At the end of his long years of faithful service, Paul was again in prison. He had given everything to Jesus and the advancement of His kingdom. For Paul, there were no regrets. He wrote his protégé, Timothy, "For I am already being poured out like a drink offering, and the time has come for my departure. I have fought the good fight, I have finished the race, I have kept the faith. Now there is in store for me the crown of righteousness, which the Lord, the righteous Judge, will award to me on that day—and not only to me, but also to all who have longed for his appearing" (2 Tim. 4:6–8 NIV 1984). Until we take our last breath, there's no limit on our potential. We keep taking the lid off at every stage of our lives. Each time, we face new challenges, but we have more resources of wisdom and strength.

NEVER TOO LATE

One of the most amazing things about God's grace is that it's never too late to turn back to Him and experience His forgiveness, love, and power. In His kindness and wisdom, He somehow weaves even our brokenness and repentance into the fabric of our lives and makes them into something beautiful. It's amazing. I've talked to many people who have concluded that they've messed up too badly for too long for God to ever bless them. I assure them that God is the God of another chance. We may experience the natural consequences of sin and dumb decisions, but God is never finished with us. He takes us as we are and makes us trophies of His grace.

I saw an illustration of this principle in my own home. Carla went on a trip for a week, and she gave me clear instructions about taking care of the house. One of the items on her list was to water a particular plant in the living room. As you might have guessed, I got busy doing other things that week, and I didn't water the plant a single time. The day before she came home, I walked by the pot. The plant looked as though it had been next to a nuclear explosion! Every leaf was brown and brittle. I was going to throw it out (and hope Carla didn't miss it). I told my mother about it, and she had some surprising advice. She said, "Just water it. I know it looks dead and hopeless, but it'll probably come back to life."

I wondered if she was pulling my leg, but I decided to follow her advice. I watered the plant and pulled off all the dead leaves. It looked even worse than before! The next morning, I walked into the living room. I looked carefully at the plant, and I noticed its stalks had started standing up again, and the buds beginning to appear on the stems were turning green again. It was alive! It wasn't going to look great by the time Carla came home that afternoon, but at least I hadn't killed her plant.

Some of us are like that plant. Our souls haven't been watered by the grace of God for a long time, so we look dead and barren. The soul-nourishing water of the Spirit and the Word can bring us back to life. Some brown and brittle leaves need to be pulled off, but soon, signs of life return. We thought hope was lost, but it never is. God always has something wonderful for us.

Job had every reason to give up on God and his future. Through a series of calamities, he lost everything—except his complaining wife. His children were killed in a freak storm, thieves stole his wealth, and his health was broken. In the middle of all this pain, his best friends blamed him for his troubles! Job had nowhere to go—nowhere except to God. In chapter after chapter, he poured out his heart. Finally, God spoke to Job and overwhelmed him with His majesty, wisdom, and power. God assured Job that his life wasn't over. The last verses in this long book in the Old Testament say, "After this, Job lived a hundred and forty years; he saw his children and their children to the fourth generation. And so he died, old and full of years" (Job 42:16–17 NIV 1984). In spite of all he had endured, God promised a fresh sense of life, love, and hope. And Job experienced the blessings of God.

BE A CHAMELEON

Our problems may not be as devastating or as sudden as Job's, but all of us face our own forms of "Job moments." If we expect God to make our lives easy, we'll blame Him for our troubles and give up on following Him. And if we expect God to fix our problems quickly, we may bail out when He takes too long to respond. Even when we combine the best of the creative mind and the strategic mind, we inevitably encounter obstacles and opposition. In these crucial times, we need to adapt and persevere. A dream may look dead, but God isn't finished with His purpose for us. If we trust Him in the darkness, He'll bring us back into the light. If we don't bail out when our dreams die, we'll be poised for a glorious future. It may not happen quickly, and it'll always be full of surprises, but restoration will happen.

In the warm climates from central Africa to south Asia, we find a most peculiar animal—one that can teach us a lot about pressing on to greater things. The chameleon is a lizard that has unusual abilities to adapt. Many of them can dramatically change colors to blend in to their surroundings. Chameleons have specialized skin cells, called *chromatophores*, containing pigments in three layers below their transparent outer skin. They appear bright green on a leaf, dark brown on a tree trunk, and even blue, red, yellow, or orange! Chameleons constantly sense the need of their environment, and they instantly adapt to fit the situation. Their adaptations may be defensive, to protect themselves from hungry predators, or they may adapt so they can snatch unsuspecting bugs for their next meal. Their tongues are often twice as long as their bodies, so they can grab insects from long distances. Chameleons also have eyes that are unique in the animal world. Their eyes can move separately on wide orbits so they can see the full 360 degrees around them without turning their heads. These eyes are stereoscopic to identify the exact distance of any threat or opportunity. Their feet, too, are uniquely designed to take advantage of their lives in the trees. They can grip almost anything, hanging on to the smallest twig or climbing the biggest trees. The creative hand of God has already given the chameleon everything it needs to adapt, survive, and thrive.

If a chameleon stopped adapting, it wouldn't last through the day! Its nature is to continually sense dangers and opportunities so it can change to meet its immediate needs and thrive another day.

Many of us are numbed by past wounds, present stresses, and the blare of constant media. God has given us His Spirit to help us perceive what's going on around us so we can adapt and respond. Unfortunately, many of us have turned this switch off on our control panels. When we don't perceive needs around us, we drift through life in a fog. Our hearts aren't thrilled with seeing God at work, we don't sense the Spirit's nudge to offer a word of kindness, and our hearts don't melt with compassion when we encounter the broken hearts of others.

It may sound strange, but I think we need to become like lizards—no, not just any lizard, but the adaptable, sensitive, responsive chameleon. The threats are all around us, tempting us to doubt God and our abilities. Our Enemy may not live in a forest canopy, but he's lethal. Satan has come to steal, kill, and destroy, so we need to be on guard and realize he's like a lion, seeking to devour us (John 10:10; 1 Peter 5:8).

Like the chameleon, we, too, have been given all we need to adapt to every situation. God's "divine power has given us everything we need for a godly life through our knowledge of him who called us by his own glory and goodness" (2 Peter 1:3). We just need to actualize the gifts, talents, and strengths He has already entrusted to us. Nothing is a surprise to God. Through Isaiah, God declared, "I make known the end from the beginning, from ancient times, what is still to come. I say, 'My purpose will stand, and I will do all that I please'" (Isa. 46:10). God has already *worked it out* while we're trying to *figure it out.* God has given us plenty of *provisions* to fulfill the *vision* He has put in our hearts. But achieving our potential is never a straight-line path. Every good drama has intrigue, plot twists, and unexpected roadblocks—and our lives are the ultimate drama in the universe. The angels are watching and cheering us on!

It's easy to coast, to drift, and to stop pressing forward. In every aspect of life, we have to keep injecting creativity and passion to pursue the next, greater dream. When I write songs, I can hear an inspiring melody, enlist outstanding musicians and vocalists, but there still may be something intangible missing. If I don't encounter the sharp edge of excellence, my song won't reach its full potential. When I'm singing, writing, or recording, I can tell if I'm on that edge or not. When I am, I sense the power of the Holy Spirit pushing me further. When I'm not, I've learned to stop, reflect, and—like the chameleon—adapt, so the song can reach its full potential.

No matter how many songs have been written and sung, there are always more beautiful ones waiting to be expressed. No matter how many hearts have been touched and people served, there are always new ways to capture them with love, grace, and strength. No matter how damaged a family may be, there's always hope for reconciliation and restoration. No matter how beautiful a marriage has become, both spouses need to keep infusing the relationship with tenderness, understanding, joy, and creativity.

Some people need to trust God for the first dramatic vision of their lives. They need to dig deep into the heart of God and find hope to wash away their despair. But others need to discover their second, third, or fourth visions and vocations. They've seen success, and they're thankful for all God has done—but they sense there's something more for them to do for God and His glory.

Don't settle for an empty life. Equally important, don't settle for a successful life. God's design is always higher, bigger, and better than we can imagine. Earlier, we looked at two passages that remind us that no one has seen, heard, or even imagined all that God wants to do in and through those who love Him (1 Cor. 2:9).

Paul ended one of his prayers with the hope-filled flourish that God "is able to do immeasurably more than all we ask or imagine, according to his power that is at work within us" (Eph. 3:20). In other words, dream big and dream again, but realize that God's dreams for you are far higher than your human imagination can grasp. He's the Creator, King, and Savior of the universe! Nothing is too difficult for Him!

There's always something deeper God wants to do in you, always more people He wants you to impact, and more blessings God wants to pour out on you. The abundant life is never a placid, complacent life. Jesus invites people: "Follow me" (see Matt. 4:19; 8:22; 9:9 NKJV). Following Him is always into the unknown, the risky, and the wonderful. But it is the adventure of a lifetime. Never stop growing. Never give up on the potential of God doing something marvelous in and through you. Never let anyone try to put the lid back on your life and hold you down.

NO LIMITATIONS

The words on your birth certificate and the picture on your driver's license don't tell the full story of your life. God created you with enormous natural talents and spiritual resources. You aren't the sum total of your past, and you aren't a prisoner of your present. You were made for more than you can imagine. There are no limitations on what God will do in you and through you if you'll trust Him, follow Him, and take the lid off your life.

Don't complain about the way things are, and don't wait for someone else to fulfill your dreams. It's your responsibility—and your high privilege—to take the initiative and take bold steps forward. Don't allow negative people to hold you back, and don't let painful circumstances erode your hopes. God hasn't just given you some abilities; He has given you His life. You are the receptacle of the matchless grace of almighty God, the temple of the Holy Spirit, a member of the anointed holy priesthood of God, and a humble servant of the mighty King. Know it. Taste it. Live it.

Paul ended his letter to the Philippians with a declaration and a promise. He told them, "I can do everything through him who gives me strength." Then, he promised, "My God will meet all your needs according to his glorious riches in Christ Jesus" (Phil. 4:13, 19 NIV 1984). All your needs? Yes, all of them. How? Not according to human limitations, but according to the vast resources of the One who created it all! It's by His calling that we know who we are and how our lives have meaning. It's by His power that great things are accomplished. It is through the wonder of His grace that He calls us His friends, sons, daughters, and heirs of the promise.

What's your next step? It's really not that difficult to discern. What has God put on your heart that you've resisted? What conversation have you put off too long? What dream is dormant in your heart? What action have you avoided out of fear? What needs have you overlooked because they seemed too big? What person have you walked past but sensed God wanted you to touch with His love? What great plan has been gathering dust in your mind because you haven't had the faith to trust God to accomplish it?

The lid of doubt and delay may look different for different people, but we all have one. It's time. Don't wait any longer. Take the lid off, and see what God will do. I guarantee you: it'll be amazing! I believe in you, but more important, God believes in you. Trust Him, love Him, and follow Him.

Character cannot be developed in ease and quiet. Only through experience of trial and suffering can the soul be strengthened, ambition inspired, and success achieved.

—HELEN KELLER

CONSIDER THESE QUESTIONS

1. What are some plateaus or goals that you have set and assumed, "When I get there, I can coast from then on"?
2. Read Philippians 3:12–15. How would you paraphrase or explain Paul's perspective? How does your view of life compare to his?
3. What are some reasons some people assume that God has given up on them and that it's too late to experience God's best? How does Job's experience help you trust God even in the darkest times?
4. What lessons can you learn from the chameleon? What are some ways you need to adapt to threats and opportunities?
5. After reading this book, how would you define what it means to "take the lid off" your life?
6. What's your next step? What has God been saying to you in this book?

ACKNOWLEDGMENTS

I COULDN'T IMAGINE WRITING MY FIRST BOOK AND NOT TAKING THE OPPORTUNITY to acknowledge and appreciate the foundation and contributions of my grandparents, the late Florine Brown-Montgomery, Mollie Freeman, Ethel Chatman, and Leroy Brown Sr.; my great-uncle, the late Lewie A. Norful Sr.; and my great-aunt, the late Ovita Freeman. Also, my grandmother Faye Neal and my great-aunt Alice Norful. And certainly, the creative motivation for this book, my great-grandmother, the late Idell Chatman.

I stand on all your sacrifices, prayers, compassion, perseverance, and yes, even your pain. Without you and all those other greats and grands whom I didn't have the pleasure of knowing in my lifetime, I would not be who I am nor have done any of what I've been blessed to do. Your triumphs fueled my belief in myself; your failures prompted my redirection; your transparency allowed for teachable moments; your candor was alarmingly helpful; your compassion soothed my soul and quieted my fears; your love taught me the meaning of unconditional; and your lives served as a guiding light to all of us. You are missed so much every single day. Thank you for believing in me, supporting me, loving me, and making sure I knew how to take the lid off. My hope is to live up to your expectations and leave for my grands and greats what you have left for me—an incredible *legacy*.

I unquestionably could not do anything I do in ministry without the greatest church family and ministry team in the world! Victory Cathedral Worship Center, you have been an amazing group of people to pastor, and you continue to amaze me with your level of faith in God and confidence in the vision of God. I love you all so dearly. And for my executive team and my entire ministry staff, I praise God! You are the guardians of the vision and architects of the mission. Your prayers, love, support, and perseverance make it all attainable and I truly couldn't do it without you.

Last, but certainly most valuable, Jason Tyson, Eugene Gatewood, Marc Smith, Marc Wells, and the rest of my VCWC leadership and staff. Your loyalty and support throughout the years is undeniable and tremendously appreciated. You are my brothers, family, and friends. Your commitment to my ministry and vision has been proven a thousand times over. For this I will be eternally grateful. My ministry could have never been what it is if not for you. I love and appreciate you with all my heart.

ABOUT THE AUTHOR

SMOKIE NORFUL IS FOUNDER AND SENIOR PASTOR OF VICTORY CATHEDRAL Worship Center, a congregation on three campuses in Bolingbrook and Chicago, Illinois. A graduate of the University of Arkansas at Pine Bluff and Trinity International University in Deerfield, Illinois, Norful also served on the board of regents for Trinity International University. A multiple Grammy-winning artist who has sold more than three million albums worldwide, he has also received Stellar awards; Dove awards; an NAACP Image Award nomination; a Soul Train Award nomination; two nominations for the BET Award for gospel music; two RIAA certified Gold-selling compact discs; and countless other awards. He lives with his wife and family in the Chicago area.

NOTES

Chapter 1: All or Nothing

1. See 2 Timothy 4:2.
2. "Great Is Thy Faithfulness," Hope Publishing Co., 1951, http://www.hopepublishing.com.
3. Os Guinness, *The Call* (Nashville: Word, 1998), 4.
4. Isaac Watts, "When I Survey the Wondrous Cross," published in 1707, public domain.
5. See Isaiah 43:25 CEV.
6. A. W. Tozer, *Fellowship of the Burning Heart* (Alachua, FL: Bridge-Logos, 2006), 19.
7. Augustine, quoted in Garry Wills, *Saint Augustine* (New York: Penguin Putnam, 1999), 139–40.

Chapter 2: Blinded by Sight

1. "All About Madonna," *Vanity Fair*, April 1991, https://allaboutmadonna.com/madonna-library/madonna-interview-vanity-fair-april-1991.
2. *Good Housekeeping*, October 1990, 87–88.
3. Mark Galli, "A Terrifying Grace," *Christianity Today*, May 24, 2013,

http://www.christianitytoday.com/ct/2013/june/terrifying-grace-god-omniscience.html.

Chapter 3: Upside Down

1. Daniel G. Amen and David E. Smith, *Unchain Your Brain: Ten Steps to Breaking the Addictions That Steal Your Life* (N.p.: MindWorks Press, 2010).
2. For much more on this concept, see Pastor Timothy Keller's article, "Life in the Upside-Down Kingdom," *Journal of Biblical Counseling* 17, no. 3 (Spring 1999), cited at www.newcityindy.org/wp-content/uploads/2009/07/Upside-Down-Kingdom.Tim-Keller.pdf.
3. H. Norman Wright, *Quiet Times for Couples* (Eugene, OR: Harvest House, 1990), 91.

Chapter 7: See It, Say It, Sense It, Seek It

1. Beth Stebner, "Workplace Morale Heads Down: 70% of Americans Negative About Their Jobs, Gallup Study Shows," *New York Daily News*, June 24, 2013, http://www.nydailynews.com/news/national/70-u-s-workers-hate-job-poll-article-1.1381297.

Chapter 8: Dream Again

1. Tom Brady, interview by Steve Kroft, *60 Minutes*, CBS, November 6, 2005, http://www.cbsnews.com/news/transcript-tom-brady-part-3/.